Shetland Crofter Postie

Shetland Crofter Postie

Davy Simmons

The Shetland Times Ltd.
Lerwick
2002

Shetland Crofter Postie

ISBN 1 898852 84 7

First published by The Shetland Times Ltd., 2002.

British Library Cataloguing-in-Publication Data
A catalogue record for this book is available from the British Library.

Printed and published by
The Shetland Times Ltd.,
Gremista, Lerwick,
Shetland ZE1 0PX, UK.

Dedicated to
my wife Jean and to the memory of our late children-in-law
Leif Einarrson and Liz Simmons (neé Le-Boutillier)

Contents

Illustrations

Part I

Seasons in the life of a Crofter Postie

Chapter 1
A Snowy Day

Gradually I awoke from the bliss of slumber to a conscious realisation that between myself and my deeply sleeping wife, lay the warm form of our youngest daughter Ruth. Sometime during the night she had crawled out of her crib and found her way between these two weary souls, both dead to the world after a hard day and a late night. It had always been the habit of our children to end up between Mam and Dad – I must say we liked it that way. Sometimes they had kicked off their covers and become cold; sometimes fear or loneliness drove them our way. What comfort the bed promises to every age, every condition; sorrow, grief and pain; joy, delight and hope; anger, spite

1. The croft at Gert.

and passion, all eclipsed and laid aside in the brief oblivion of the night watches. The king and the slave, the condemned and the exalted, all unaware for a little space of time of the world and its ways, the coming day with all it may hold or promise.

I rolled over and took the slumbering infant in my arms, conscious of the warmth of her little body against me and her steady hot breath upon my face, thus enjoying another brief moment. This luxury was but for a blink as I knew that it was now ten to six, no need of an alarm clock, early call or cock crow; for years every morning, winter and summer, I awoke within a minute of ten to six. Of course, when "the powers that be" altered the clock in the summer, my internal clock didn't alter to their dictates but awoke me at its own time, being an hour earlier; but as there was always much to do during our brief summer, the extra hour was a kind of blessing.

I kissed the little cheek and rose from my warm cocoon, dressing in the chill and darkness of the little bedroom with its coomb ceiling, small skylight and slightly larger window. Making my way down the stairs and into the warmth of the kitchen with its mixed smell of peat reek, drying fish, reestit mutton and a pillowcase full of kale seed heads, which should have been dealt with months previously, I wasn't surprised, when, putting down the switch, no light appeared, as a heavy northerly gale with snow had been blowing all night, hence no electrical power. "Well," thought I, "this is nothing new." After groping around I found the matches and lit the oil lamps and a candle, raked out the ash from the Trueburn and fired in some dry sticks and peats. Within a minute it was roaring up the lum, as in those days we always rested the fire at night by putting ash on the glowing peats. Pulling the kettle over to the hottest end of the stove, I made for the byre, pail and cloth in hand (a white enamel pail made in Russia – a gift from my friend Laurie Anderson).

As I bent low through the five-foot door joining the kitchen with the outbuildings, I said, "May the dear Lord have blessed the soul that thought to put house, barn, byre, ram house and hen house all under one roof." For in complete comfort one could move from the but-end to the byre in a pair of smucks, only then putting on one's byre boots on the wildest of nights, without poking your nose out of doors.

Of course this house design had its origins among the Viking people with their "long houses" and that design was retained right up to modern times. Having come through the first low door, one was immediately confronted with a second door of the same dimensions. The first door opening

2. The but-end.

as stated into the kitchen (but-end), the second door opening into the barn, thus creating a passage of less than four feet through the drystone gable of the house. This second door swung on wooden hinges, common in all croft houses a century before but somewhat less common in the era in which I am now writing. The light from the flickering candle illuminated the low barn with its hay loft ceiling just above one's head, into this loft we stored enough hay and sheaves to last the animals at least a month. This fodder was forked up through a large door in the south gable of the loft from the yard below. This loft arrangement was not so common in barns in Shetland. The house and buildings ran North and South, the house being at the North end. The beginning of each winter would display a pleasing sight in the yard of several skroos (corn stacks), desses of hay, large coles of ryegrass and long triangular heaps of neaps and swedes neatly covered with straw and möld (earth).

Behind all this was row after row of Shetland kale stalks, all the results of long hours of summer and hairst toil.

The contents of the barn were those which would have been found in nearly every barn in Shetland at that period, an assortment of hoes, rakes, Shetland spades, spades, shovels, pick and crowbar, two or three tuskars, a ripper, meshies, bales of kyaar, nets, kishies and fishing gear; an A.35 van and our faithful old petrol paraffin tractor, both attended to with love and care only appropriate to a sick child, not to two pieces of machinery. Two large tattie crös ran a third way along the west side of the barn and were filled to the ceiling with "Kerr's Pink" tatties. A wooden partition separated the barn from the byre, along which was built a large box affair, where two or three days supply of neaps and kale were stored. Through this maze of machinery, crofting and fishing gear I made my way to the byre door.

In the byre a blast of snow-laden air was soaring heavenwards from one of the ventilation holes above Blackie's head, the snow falling lightly down upon her wide back. "Serves dee right, du gluttonous brute. If du had left yon hay alone dat I stuffed in da vent da streen (last night), du would have been as warm and snug as the rest o da beasts. Du's a witless object." The other four kye and six young animals all lay quietly in their cramped quarters. Cramped because I had taken out the front wall of the byre the previous summer and extended it out six feet, building up the new front wall with six inch blocks, only bringing it to a height of five feet, so as not to alter the pitch of the extended roof. A simple alteration but a bit low above the heads of the young beasts.

I slapped the backside of June, a little black and white Shetland coo, the smallest one I have seen in recent times, more like those I remember as a boy at Gulberwick. Her mother came from Jim Moncrieff, Urafirth. The Shetland bull was one Bertie Moar of Murrister kept. We kept June for thirteen years, after that she would not hold to calf, so she went the way of all old kye – Tony Anderson or Aberdeen Marts. Her fate was Aberdeen and I only cleared £30 for her; she was so small.

She rose, I wiped her udder and paps and sat me down on the three legged stool with the pail between my knees and my forehead pushed hard into her warm flank. Now the warm milk was sploshing in long streaks into the pail, causing a froth to rise. At the sound of the milk on the inside of the pail, Miss Ninky came running and meowing for her share. I had, as ever, taken Ninky's "Fray Bentos steak and kidney pie" tin with me, which now lay between coo and stool. Into this I squirted Ninky's breakfast and she happily lapped away. When finished she purred and fawned around the calf of my leg, begging a little more. What a scene of tranquillity and peace a little low Shetland byre is, lit only with a single wick oil lamp nailed to a stanchion between the runnick and the young animals. It was the kind of lamp with a round metal reflector at the back of the glass globe, throwing a good light forward but shadowed behind, obscuring the young beast in darkness. Once June had given her lot – about a gallon – I baaled a sheaf of "Ayr Bounty Oats" to the muckle kye and half a sheaf of corn to the young ones. Also a good kale stalk to June. Jean would water them later. By the time the milking was by, all the kye, young and old, were to their feet and enjoying their corn o maet.

Blowing out the lamp in the byre, I lit the storm lantern, made my way to the hen house which was attached to the westside of the barn, and poured mixed corn into their trough, lighting their little oil lamp (the light promotes egg laying in the dark days of winter). The hens remained on their reest so I left them, hoping the mice would not beat them to their breakfast. Once the ram was fed I passed on through the barn and into the but-end.

The kettle was boiling fiercely, the room was fine and warm and in no time I was sitting enjoying a meagre repast – a Black's Water biscuit and a mug of sweet tea. The lamp threw deep and strange shadows in the little kitchen, making the shadows of reestit mutton hanging from the hooks in the ceiling look like fists, heads and sails. I thought how warm and hamely it all was and how uninviting the prospects outside the walls of our little croft house were on this wild, bleak and snowy morning.

I carried up a cup of tea, biscuit and candle to my sleeping wife telling her I was for off in fifteen minutes, just enough time for a "fill up" and a short read of the "Good Book". Back in the kitchen with cup in one hand and Bible in the other I read a little from the Book of Proverbs, as the hands of the clock crept slowly up to five to seven. Once there, I put on the Post Office tie, jacket and carcoat (the best article of clothing the Post Office ever supplied), buttoned this up to below my chin, pulled on my oilskin breeks over the normal ones, took out the warm gloves from the lower shelf of the Trueburn oven and completed my dress by donning the new lugged leather cap Jean had made me the week before. Once attired I turned down the lamp, picked up the blinkie (torch), closed the but-end door and once in the darkened passage I could just distinguish the faint light of the candle from the bedroom. Calling up to Jean not to send the bairns to the school unless the weather was greatly improved by 9am, which was very unlikely, I also told her I didn't expect to make it back from Waas (Walls) for my breakfast before 10.30am, if then.

At that time in my career as a postie I was employed part-time, entailing the pick up of the outgoing mail from the Sandness Post Office at Melby, then three times a week, weather permitting, collecting and leaving mail in the shed at the Melby pier or, if the Papa Stour mail boat was in Sandness, receiving the outgoing mail from John Jamieson. Taking this outgoing mail to Walls, from where it would be transported into Lerwick by a van which, on its outward journey from Lerwick, would have put off incoming mail to the various Post Offices between Lerwick and Waas (Walls) including Skeld, Reawick and Bridge of Walls. Once I had delivered the outgoing mail to the Lerwick van, the mail, letters, parcels and so on for Sandness had to be sorted in the Waas Post Office. On this operation being completed I would make my way back to Sandness, have my breakfast and commence my delivery. This is how things were wrought at the time I am now relating. We will now continue with my story.

3. The author's Post Office van making its way through the snow on the Sandness road.

Switching on my blinkie I moved into the porch where I stood, hoping the snow would ease as it swirled around the weather side of the porch. As I stood there the cold began to penetrate my very being. So without further ado I went out into a swirling blizzard and a January morning as black as pitch. (Much later in my employment with the Post Office we were told in such conditions to remain at home until the snow ploughs had opened up the main road, but certainly not at this juncture. Now we just don't get these kind of winters.)

I had left the van as close to the dyke around the house as possible, so it was but seconds before I was getting the windscreen clear of snow and clambering into the Morris van. At no time was she any trouble to start and true to form she spluttered into life at the first touch of the starter. For the next five minutes or so I kept the window wiper and engine running, getting warmth into the system until there was enough hot air to get rid of the ice on the inside and outside of the windscreen. Once clear I was off; the Gert road,

4. Gert on a winter's day.

running down to the main road runs north and south so little snow was able to lie there but once I turned into the main road to the westward it was a different story. Deep fans (drifts) kept me busy until I reached the mill brae. There the fans were much deeper but being on a steep downward gradient I charged through them in third gear and at top speed. This I enjoyed greatly and hitting the fan at that speed generally carried the van through short fans as much as five feet high. One struck the fan at 30mph, (it was like striking head-on a large sea in a small boat but instead of green seas breaking over the boat, it was a white wall of snow) but before all the way (motion, speed) was taken off, the van was clear and careering down towards the next fan, the wipers having a hard job to provide vision even at top wiper speed.

Once on the flat and uphill it was a case of digging one's self through until two miles on and a half an hour's work later I was at the Post Office. After getting the mailbag from both the office and the Papa store I headed on my long journey to Waas through the bleak hills. Outside the Turriefield grind (gate) to the Waas turn-off there were at that time seventy-two bends. The road up the steep hill at Tronisgord again runs more or less north and south and the snow being driven with a force nine gale hadn't allowed much snow to drift, blowing it out over the tops of the hills. Every hilltop was bearing, filling the valleys and broos with a great depth of snow and burying many sheep. The evidence of this would only show up in the crangs (carcasses) of the many sheep which had not been located and dug up once the weather had moderated.

The fans I encountered up Tronisgord and to Bankard's Corner were navigated through, either by top speed assaults or by digging in the midst of this moorie caavie (snowstorm). At Bankard Corner I with great reluctance dragged out the chains, ran the back wheels over into the middle of them and, lying on my back in the snow, with frozen fingers at last managed to get them fastened around the wheels. By then I resembled a snowman. I again got seriously stuck at Faroeman's corner just past the top of Storburgh Hill. The corner takes its name from a young Faroese man by the name of Magnus Joanneson who flew off the road late one dark winter's night in a Mini at great speed and had seven miles to walk, without seeing a single car all the way into Sandness, to get help. Six of us went back and got the car carried and pushed back upon the road.

It took me an hour to break through this long deep fan, digging and then setting the van in gear, pulling out the choke to maintain revs on the engine.

5. *Typical conditions on the Sandness road. At a later date than events in this book.*

I would jump out of the van and, standing outside the door of the van, shove and steer until she was free, then smartly leap aboard before I lost her, to keep her going until she was clear of the fan or again stuck.

At that time I was always first out of Sandness in the mornings – Jim Peterson and others following shortly after – but I was the only man that morning foolish enough to be on the road. I didn't attempt to go down the Brunertwatt road for I knew from past experience it would be impossible. So I carried on digging and shuffling to the main Lerwick – Waas road. At the Brig O Waas junction I stopped and peered through the blizzard and lo and behold saw a snow plough coming down towards the Brig O Waas and behind it a car and the Lerwick Post van. As they passed I joined the convoy and came safely into Waas. It had taken me just over three hours to cover eleven miles, if one counts the two miles detour into Melby to pick up the mail. I asked the snowplough driver if he would clear the Sandness road and, once in Sandness, at least clear the Bousta road so that I could at last get home for my breakfast, which was duly done plus the road to Huxter and the Post Office.

Speaking of Huxter, it was at Huxter some years before the event I am relating, that Jimmy Georgeson noticed a quitraat (stoat) eyeing up some small birds feeding on the seeds of grasses and dead dockens which were sticking up through the snow. After some time, the quitraat made its way over the snow covered ground and buried itself amongst the stalks of grasses and dockens and by now, all that Jimmy could see was the white tail with its black tip standing erectly out of the snowy waste. After some little time the birds returned to their feeding, flitting from stalk to stalk until at last one of the flock landed on the erect tail. In a moment there was an explosion of snow as the quitraat sprang into the air, seizing the unsuspecting bird, and in a split second it was all over. The flock fled, leaving their hapless companion to its fate. Wondrous are the ways of God in providing for His creatures.

The countless myriad's of terrestrial beings, from man the head, to the creeping insect at the foot, are all supported and nourished by the Divine bounty. As is the case of the peerie swaabie (lesser black-backed gull) that for years in the month of May and June has patrolled the Ness and Veltegert lochs, snatching up any unfortunate eel that ventures into the shallow waters of two feet or less. This the dextrous creature achieves while still on the wing, carrying its prize to the nearest bank, where it then commences to peck and thrash it upon the ground, while the lively eel does its utmost to regain the safety of the loch. After some time the swaabie seems to tire of its efforts and swallows the writhing eel down with great difficulty. Most of its catches seem to be about nine inches long, though I saw it catch an eighteen incher – that one was swallowed and disgorged so many times I got tired watching it and eventually left the scene, for as one may know an eel takes a lot of killing and will wriggle minus its head for long enough.

It was here in Waas that the last case of leprosy was ever recorded in the British Isles, a small leper house having been built outside the dykes of the toonship to house these unfortunate people.

It is a pity so much of the local history has been lost throughout Shetland, for had it been recorded, it would have made very interesting reading. So often it's the tragic that is remembered, the pleasant and amusing forgotten. As was the case of one of the sheep thieves of Waas, who had noticed a fine fat hog lamb tethered on the green behind a crofter's house at the far end of the parish. Once darkness had fallen, it being the month of October, he set out to execute his crime and on his arrival at the croft he was delighted to find that a gimmer lamb had now been brought home from the hill to be company for the hog, both being cringed together (cringed – two animals on one tether which takes on the appearance of the letter Y, a swivel being placed where the two legs of the Y meet). He quickly tied the legs of both lambs with sufficient rope between the two to enable him to drape the lambs over his shoulders, and take the weight of them on the rope across his chest. After he had travelled about a mile towards his own home, he came to the dykes of Bardister, where he set the two lambs on the top of the dyke while he took a rest – still having the rope across his chest. The lambs at this point must have struggled and slipped over the other side of the dyke, drawing the rope up from his chest and around his throat. The next morning folk on their way to the Kirk (it being Sunday) found that Divine Justice had taken place during the night watches and the notorious thief was no more, thus saving the people of Waas the job of escorting the villain to "Gallowhill". The lambs were returned to their owner, where they contentedly pecked (grazed) the grass behind the house, none the worse for spending a few hours upside down.

One that did end up on Gallowhill was Bartholomew Reid (Bastie Reid for short). Gibby Law was a wandering tailor, going from home to home in the execution of his lawful trade. On the day of his death he left Sandness for his next appointment which was at Browster, Bridge of Waas, a distance of about seven miles. He called at the house of Kellister for rest and a bite to eat. He also had another reason for breaking his journey and that was to collect money owed to him by the Reid couple. The debt was duly paid and put into the tin box which he carried upon his back. This box contained the tools of his trade plus payments for work he had completed. Gibby parted from the Reids in good humour and proceeded on his way.

Bastie and his wife had seen the little money contained in the box and decided to steal it by hook or by crook. Gibby had a defect in his make up for he was born blind in one eye and Bastie took advantage of this fact. Stealthily he stole up to his intended victim on his blind side, striking him a terrible blow with his spade on the crown of his head. With that single blow he ushered Gibby into eternity, whether Heaven or Hell one cannot say. We may trust it was the former. Gibby's constant companion was his little dog and had it not fled away from this brutal man, it would no doubt have suffered a similar fate. Bastie then used his weapon of death to hide his sinful crime by digging a grave in the moor at the side of the burn, which from then on carries the name of the slain Gibby Law's Burn. Into this he dumped the poor tailors body. What Bastie's thoughts were we will never know, whether remorse, callous indifference or satisfaction at having gained his objective, who knows. But Scripture states "For what shall it profit a man, if he shall gain the whole world and lose his own soul? Or what shall a man give in exchange for his soul?" Mark 8 : 36 & 37.

The failure of Gibby to keep his appointment at Browster was soon noticed and a general search was made of the hills between Sandness and the Bridge of Waas. At last his little dog was found sitting on the spot where his late master lay buried. The body was soon exhumed and carried to the Waas Kirk, where the elders and minister assembled to decide what was to be done. After some debate it was decided to make every person in the Sandness and Walls districts, approach and look on the face of the dead man under the scrutiny of the minister and elders. When at length it came for Bastie Reid to come forward, the blind eye of Gibby Law opened and looked fully at Bastie, as a drop of blood rolled down the deceased's cheek. (One can believe that if you like.) Something about the behaviour of the murderer prompted his arrest, he was thereupon taken to the gallow hill and hung. He was then beheaded and the head was taken around each home in the district as a solemn warning against such a dastardly and heinous crime against such a harmless and peaceable soul. His wife was also taken and hanged, being party to her husbands' wickedness.

One murder that was not punished as far as this world is concerned, is that of the fourteen year old boy Gabriel Jamieson, born in 1867, murdered 1881. His mother was unmarried and they lived in the Dale of Waas and at the time of the boy's death they were staying in Norby, Sandness. It is likely that the mother was helping out at some confinement or at a sick bed. With regard to the woman's family in Dale there was said to be ill blood between the mother's folk in Dale and a very ill tempered crofter from the same place. Gabriel was said to have killed a lamb or two of this disagreeable and violent man. The man in the presence of others stated he would cut off the head of Gabriel Jamieson if he ever caught him near his sheep, the same as the boy had done to his lambs. It must be said at this juncture that Gabriel was a very bad and cruel boy having cut off the heads of some young birds, the child was really quite wicked but this did not justify the end he met.

In the month of August, Gabriel's mother sent him over to Dale from Sandness, a distance of approximately three and a half miles. That afternoon the people in Huxter, Sandness were working on the corn rigs when they heard a distant distinct cry far away in the hill and then silence. This unusual sound left the group of crofters mystified but unfortunately no further action was taken. Had an investigation been made they would likely have seen the murderer dragging the lifeless body to the cliffs. Meanwhile Gabriel's mother was not alarmed when her son didn't return to Sandness that evening after delivering the errand she had sent him with but when he didn't return the next day she went over to Dale to her mother's house to see what had become of him. She was then told the boy had never been in Dale, whereupon she became very anxious for his wellbeing. A search was then made but he was not to be found. Some little time later Waas men were coming from the "far haaf" (a fishing which was carried on 30 to 50 miles off shore) when they discovered a headless body floating in the Papa Sound. This they landed at Snareness, Sandness and it was identified as Gabriel Jamieson's remains. This was reported to the authorities in Lerwick and the said crofter was investigated, but no charge was made as the evidence was only circumstantial, but the local people both in Sandness and Dale knew only too well whom the murderer was. His name is still known to some of us older ones even today. Justice will one day be done, for the Good Book states "after death the Judgement."

Another true tale but with a happier ending is told of a man who, on leaving one of the many shops that Waas once boasted with his errands for the weekend, was caught in a very severe blizzard. With wind over 100mph and powder-like snow, he did the only thing possible in such circumstances and went before the blizzard not knowing where he was. At length he found a slight break from the storm on the lee side of a large peat stack and as the lee side was very quickly filling up with snow, he decided to get inside of the stack. Fortunately there had been a night of rain followed by a very severe frost prior to the blizzard, which made the outside of the stack as firm as the side of a house. He soon made a hole large enough for him to crawl into, and once in the heart of the peat stack, he built in the entrance with the peats from inside, enlarging his snug shelter until he was able to lie his length in comfort, while the storm raged outside. At home great alarm was in the breast of his wife and family as they thought of the fate of their dear one. He, of course, was as safe as at his own fireside, sustained by the contents of his bag, warm and about to settle down to a good night's rest. On awakening in the early hours of the next morning, he was aware that the gale had ceased and on making a small hole through the weather side of his "peaty home", he saw a clear sky dotted with stars. Now satisfied that the storm was over, he rolled over and knew nothing more, until the first streaks of a new day showed through the small hole, whereupon he took away the entrance he had built, cleared the snow that had moored up during the night and made his way home to a royal welcome.

I must now come back to my story.

Peter Williamson and Andrew Hughson, the Waas postmen, had fought their way down to the Post Office, being unable to get the vans onto the road, Waas being very full of snow. We soon had the outgoing and incoming mails dealt with, I think this was the year that no contact with the island of Foula was made from just before Christmas until the first week in March. By then the office was stapped full with mailbags for Foula, not that there hadn't been many opportunities for the boat to get out and back during that time. The trouble lay with the crew and the time of day they rose, not the weather. Today the folk on Foula would be very concerned if one week went by without contact and would class it as an emergency if it had been a month, let alone over nine weeks – but I never heard any fuss made on that occasion.

Charlie Laurenson was the Lerwick van driver that day and told us he had not gone into Skeld or Reawick as the road, he had been told at Bixter, was completely impassable. After sorting the mail, John Reid the sub-postmaster had a cup of coffee and biscuits ready for us. After being warmed inside and out I left for Sandness, the other postmen waiting for another snowplough to begin clearing the roads around Waas and Dale. It was still a very bad day and as I now had the wind and snow full in the front of the van I was anxious to catch up with the snowplough making for Sandness. I returned the way I had come via the Brig O Waas, and was surprised how quickly the road was filling in since the plough had gone through. I could see very little and was wishing I had not left Waas as things were getting much worse.

At last I caught up with the plough at the Girsy loch, a little past the Waas/Sandness junction, as they had had a tough job breaking through there. I had only just got through hours before, now a lot more snow had moored up since then. Sticking close to the back of the plough I at last made Sandness and arrived in for my breakfast at 1pm, not having delivered any mail. I was thankful to see that the bairns were at home and said I would take my breakfast and that when I returned after the delivery we would all sit down to a late dinner together. I soon consumed my usual meal – porridge, bacon, egg, a slice of mealy and currant pudding, toast and tea. Before leaving I went into the byre and flung a kale stalk to each of the kye, then off into my van and around the folk with the letters. The wind had moderated considerably and the snow was now only coming in heavy showers which were less frequent and somewhat lighter.

I did not deliver any of the letters where the roads had not been cleared by the snowplough, as it was long past my normal finishing time and I also was in a scad to get home and attend to the outside chores. Of course, the talk at every house as I came to with the mail was the snow, it had come completely unexpectedly, the previous day being fine with a cold northerly wind about force four. John Jamieson had come over with the mail from Papa Stour, taking the ingoing mail from the shed and leaving the outgoing mail, which that morning I had picked up. The great hope among the folk was that the snow would not last long, though I pointed out more than once that the signs were that it would last a while. The fact that the snow was right down to the water's edge all along the coast and the abundance that winter of snowy fools (snow buntings) were further indications. Other folk thought we were in for a 1947 snow, but as the great snow of '47 only started in February I couldn't see its connection.

It was during this winter, 1968, that we experienced the worst blizzard recorded since 1927. That particular morning broke very fine with clear skies and a light northerly wind and as usual I set off for Waas on my daily post run. On arrival we all sorted the mail and were stowing the parcels and letters into our vans, when Bertie Jamieson, the sub-Postmaster, phoned from Sandness to warn us not to leave the Waas post office as a very severe blizzard had just broken on Sandness. Within two minutes of the phone call it struck Waas. The wind was due north and a full gale of approximately 100mph, with immense quantities of powder like snow which moored up everything within minutes, a real blinnd moorie. The roads throughout Shetland were all impassable within an hour. As it was impossible to see for the blinding powder-like snow, things were extremely dangerous and great concern was expressed for anyone caught in the blizzard.

I myself was very anxious as I knew my children would be on their way to school. We didn't have the phone in those days so no contact could be made. My wife had sent two of our children off to school as usual and they had just met up with their school pal Jeffrey Cheyne at the end of our road, when the storm broke. So sudden was it that one moment it was a lovely winters morning, the next it was a blinding blizzard. My wife Jean was left holding our youngest child Ruth, praying the children could make it to Milhaugh a quarter of a mile away, or some other house, as it was impossible for them to turn for home. Our eldest daughter Kathleen was constantly being blown off her feet and was in a very distressed state but at last, with the help of her brother David, they arrived at Windyhill and David and Kathleen were taken into the house. Meanwhile Jeffrey got parted from them, but by holding on to the fence he at last arrived at the school, but was unable to say what had happened to the other two. This news when it arrived at Waas was very worrying to me as nothing could be done either from Waas or Sandness. Thankfully late in the afternoon I got a phone call to say Paul Hawkins had made contact with them and had told my wife and given her some help with the kye. It wasn't until the next day that I was able to make my way back to Sandness, when the snowplough with great difficulty opened up the Sandness road. Although only one person perished in the blizzard many came near to it on land and sea, including the late Laurie Garriock and his crew man Malcolm Robertson, it being only the preserving hand of the Almighty and the skill of the skipper that at last got them into their desired haven.

To get back to the day being related, I thought those with stock in the hill were rightly concerned for them, and I guessed that long waands (bamboo canes) and shovels would be the order of the day on the morrow, trusting the sheep buried would be found and found alive. Otherwise the cra (crow) or corby (raven) would fare well once all the snow was by. All had long given up hope of seeing me with the letters that day; tea was offered at every house but declined on account of the haste to get finished. At last I completed my Post Office duties for another day and wended my weary way back home.

The daylight would have gone that afternoon at 3.30pm but for the fact of the snow that lit the scene. I had made ready the night before (as was the normal practice) a bag of hay and a kishie (willow basket) of small maet for the sheep (tatties, neaps, kale and bruised oats). This along with a square mouth shovel I carried up to the sheephouse which at one time had been the upper house O-Gert. At one gable-end a lean-to building had been erected, a gap in the gable joining the two buildings into one, lengthening the building considerably. Around the inside walls I had built hay racks with troughs below these racks, the door was in the west gable and this had been made in two halves, allowing the upper half to be closed once the sheep were in feeding. This innovation prevented a lot of the bad weather from coming in. The open lower half allowed the sheep free access in or out. Once I had packed the racks with hay and the troughs with "smaa maet" I counted in the hame flock, – 78, 79, 80 – two missing. I called and better called but no response. After ten minutes digging in a large fan by the yard dyke I found them both and once free from their snowy prison they lost no time making for the sheep house. Theirs would only be hay that night. At first I had thought the two of them had likely gone with the sea, as when called the sheep had come up from the beach, where they had been eating waar (seaweed) and as there was a big sea running, I thought "a sea had taken them off," which is so often the case.

After this I made my way down to the byre intending to muck it out before going in, so was pleasantly surprised to find Jean had seen to that in the afternoon, while I was on the delivery around Sandness. In the porch I shed all my wet gear and made my way into the but-end where a good hot meal awaited me. A big pot of tattie soup and a pudding. What a blessing it was to have all the bairns gathered around us at the table – healthy, hungry and happy. I thought Güid grant it may always be so. The meal over, I read them a portion from the Bible as was our nightly habit and committed them to the grace of God. The reading and praying over they went about their own thing by the light of the tilley lamp and the warmth of the Trueburn. The great thing about the Trueburn over the Rayburn was the fact you could open the fire door and enjoy the cheery blaze behind the front bars. If one opens the Rayburn fire door it either reeks the house out or the thing goes out; how often have I wished we had kept the Trueburn.

Taking the pail and cloth I went through the little door in the gable-end of the kitchen and on through to the byre, milked little June, examined the bones and udder of Pinehoulland, the coo we bought from Pinehoulland in Waas, and saw much to my regret I would have to rise through the night, she being ready to calve at any time. I gave them a good skirt of excellent green hay, neaps, a few small tatties and a salt mackerel each, hung up the pail of milk out of Ninky-cat's way and sat on the milking stool at the end of the byre for half an hour, just to enjoy watching the kye contentedly eating their supper by the soft light of the oil lamp. A warm and hamely atmosphere better felt than telt, many a night I would sit there after feeding the kye.

Thankfully our byre had a concrete floor and standings between each coo, for I could remember some byres with just an earthen floor and the muck heaped up against the back wall. This all being carried out in the voar (spring) and spread upon the land. The only daylight in our byre filtered through a very small skylight and an equally small pane in the south gable. In addition to these a strip of glass had been inset above the door. Of course in fine weather we always left the door open to the delight of the hens and guinea-fowl as they picked up the oat puckles from around and between the kye's feet. Also those puckles which had passed through the kye and now resided in the runnick. I suppose they were, as one might say partly cooked! There were few puckles that ever passed through the young animals undigested.

With severe gales it was necessary to open the skylight if there was a fear of the byre roof lifting, as it tended to equalize the pressure within and outside the byre. I often had an anxious night fearing the roof would be torn off, one would see the whole of the roof, as it were, breathing in the tremendous flans of wind coming down from the Kame O Gert at the back of the house. More than once I put heavy ropes over the roof and fastened weights at both ends. Some job on a bad night, but one slept more soundly when everything moveable was well lashed down. There were few articles kept in the byre other than a stiff broom, wheelbarrow and square shovel. The calf pen at the north end of the byre was divided into two compartments, one for the calf and the other was filled with peat möld, which was used to bed down the kye at night. The möld and division was taken away as the other calves arrived. Once the third calf was born the first calf was evicted and ran around the byre at will, receiving an occasional kick when it tried to suck the wrong mother.

In the twartbaaks (tiebeams between two rafters) we always stored the piltock waands (fishing rods) and möld scrapers. The peat möld (peat dust) was scraped up from among old peat banks (möldie bletts) in the summer and used in hen, lamb, ram houses and byres to keep them dry and clean. This job was undertaken during good weather in the summer, a bit of a dusty occupation but enjoyable away from it all in the hill on a good day. Before I rose I noticed "Pinehoulland" tramping with her back legs so I hoped she would come soon and let me get to bed without having to rise in the night. I took in the milk but left the lamp burning in the byre. Jean soon had that syed (filtered) and the pail washed ready for the morning milking.

I went out of the house to see what like the night was, the wind was right down and other than the odd fluckera (large lazy snow flake) it had stopped snowing. There was a beautiful show of the merry dancers (northern lights) in the north sky stretching from NE to NW, brilliant red and the softest of green. I went in and called Jean and the bairns to see the beautiful sight, stating "the wind will fly into the NE the morn", which is often the case when the Merry Dancers are red. The cold at last drove us indoors, Jean to her maakin (knitting) yoke jumpers to Caldwell, six a week, the bairns to their toys and drawing and me to my reading of "War and Peace" by Count Tolstoy. What outstanding writers the Russians are, the likes of Dostoyevsky, Turgenev, Sholokhar, Solzhenistyn and many more were giants in Russian classic literature. So sad so few read them as they rank amongst the foremost in world literature. If we so appreciate it in English, what must it be in Russian, for usually much is lost in translation. One might ask how would Hardy, Trollope or Austin with their supreme grasp of the English language come over in Russian, would Trollope with his extravagance of description, translate into another language and still retain its rich wealth? It is likely that some of its glory would be lost.

I read on until 8pm then went into the byre while Jean got the bairns to bed. The young beasts were all lying down, the muckle kye standing and looking expectantly for their water. This last chore complete I was about to go out of the byre door when I noticed the first movements of a calf inside Blackie. The two pails of ice cold water she had drunk made him or her kick. I thought, "that's another blessing", for I was beginning to think she wasn't in calf. I had intended if I saw no signs in another week or so, to put my arm up her back passage and feel beyond her pelvis and find out for certain what the case was, so that saved me that dirty job. Outside, the northern lights were filling the heavens with a blaze of light. I was awed by the splendour of the majestic scene, translucent curtains of green and red light hanging from the black velvet of the night, now changing to great columns of crystalline rays filling the sky to the crown of heaven. Little wonder Psalm 19 begins with the words: "The heavens declare the glory of God and the firmament sheweth his handywork. Day unto day uttereth speech and night unto night sheweth knowledge." Jean and Robert came out for a look at that moment, the other three being all tucked up in bed.

At ten o'clock I took another look in at the byre and all the kye young and old (11 in total) were lying down except Pinehoulland, she was standing swishing her tail and moving from foot to foot. "You'll not be long now my lady," I thought and went outside again. I saw the heavenly show was fading so made my way in, had a wash and went to bed, setting the alarm for 11.30pm. Within moments of getting to bed sleep overcame me, only to be rudely awoken by the alarm. How easily I could have switched off the source of my annoyance, rolled over and slept the sleep of the just, but I had to rise. Turning on the blinkie I clawed on my breeks, pulled on a gansie, pushed my feet into a pair of smucks and sleepily made my way to the byre and lit the lamp. The coo was down and nose and one front foot of the unborn calf was showing. Fine, I thought, and cleaned up around the back of the coo and put down a good shovel of peat möld (dust) about her. I knelt down on a plastic bag in the runnick behind her and with some difficulty fished up the other front leg, my only thought was to get her calved as quickly as possible and get back to bed. Attaching two ropes above the kleves of the calf's feet I waited until the coo began to push again, hauling with all my strength the head came a little. I decided to get Jean up to give me a hand, five minutes later we were hauling in unison and before long we had a fine quey calf. I dragged it up to its mother who rose and was soon licking it vigorously. Once it was to its feet I steered it to the pap (what a job), made sure it got a good suck then opened the calf pen next to the coo and pushed it in and gave the coo a pail of water, as both kye and ewes are often thirsty after giving birth.

In days gone by we would have made up a drink for the coo, about half a gallon of her first milk, tea, oatmeal, brown sugar and molasses. Most kye would readily drink this; it was a safeguard against milk fever and undoubtedly saved many a coo's life, the first milk being full of calcium. Of course, this and pumping up the udder through the paps with a cycle or foot pump are preventions of the past. I blew out the lamp, closed the byre door, went on through the barn, but-end and on to bed for a few hours rest, thankful for every mercy. As we climbed into bed, Ruth climbed out of her crib and in between us. Looking back I think it's a bit dangerous to have an infant between two tired folk but thankfully she is still to the fore. Rolling over to go to sleep I said to Jean, "here ends a seasonal day in a Shetland postie's life."

Chapter 2
Voar and Summer

It is now a less severe time of year, a time when lambs, primroses, spring squill, marsh marigold and daffodils force their brave heads above the still cold sterile earth. When the skylark ascends to do homage at heaven's gate, the sweet voice of the blackbird sings from the barn roof, heralding a new season to the year's calendar. The little wren twitters in his high shrill note telling all-comers to keep clear, this is my terrain for the summer. The hill is full of curlew, whimbrel and pipit, filling the, until now, lonely and deserted waste with joyous cries of spring.

And so it was as I left the strange mystical and wondrous realm of dreamland to open my eyes to a new day, a sunny day, a voar (spring) day of

6. Kathleen on the back of her pony at Gert.

joyous delight. To be transported in a moment of time from the pleasures of sleep, the mysteries of a subconscious stupor, to the glory and light of a new spring morrow. What care I if our northern spring arrives three months after it does in the Mediterranean, or two months later than the south of England, or lags four weeks behind Scotland. It's here in the end of May in all its freshness; gone is that vehement east wind of three weeks duration burning off the new grass like a scorching flame. This ill wind's only virtue has been to dry up the new cut peats and the watery hill, to the detriment of every thing inner dykes (the crofting land inside the hill dykes), the lean new lambed ewe picking the very earth for vegetation to keep that precious little life stream of milk flowing from pap to lamb. The mothering instinct compelling her to forage day and night to rear a lamb for the slaughter.

What of the time? 10 to 5 o'clock states the timepiece on the wall, but my faithful valet within knows no British Summertime or double summertime, he wakes his lord and master at ten to six, his time, which only corresponds with their time from October to March. So, wide-awake, I ponder at leisure that which is before me, and that which has now passed and become history. From childhood I have nearly always awoken, bright, relaxed and happy. How different our waking hour is, some are so asleep they go through the first hour in a stupor, others are fine if the weather is good, others are ready for all that the world can fire at them after they have smoked their first cigarette. My late twin brother was averse to seeing or speaking to a soul in the hour of awakening. How different we all are.

What did I ponder upon my bed that May morning? Was it the goodness of a merciful heavenly Father, the great creator of all things; was it the interests of my family; was it the croft, my main interest (as far as work was concerned) with its ups and downs, its hard work and poor returns (for it was a natural and good way of life, not a profitable living), its joys and sorrows, its sense of achievement, a sense of satisfaction, its friendship with those like-minded, the common interest of all peasant folk the world over, seedtime and harvest and all that lies between; how soon has Shetland's peasant culture disappeared?

After half an hour of this reminiscing or planning, whatever it may have been, I flung back the covers, sat on the bed edge and pulled on my socks being the first act of dressing. Once all was complete I clomped down the narrow steep stair to the bathroom to perform my daily ablutions and shave the persistent and tireless growth from upon my face. What nonsense this

7. *Outside the house at Gert. From left: David-Andrew, Ruth, the author, Robert and Kitty.*

ritual is. I once grew a beard and was criticised for it, it would have remained but for the fact I trimmed it while in a dwaam (day dream), made a mess of it and shaved it off, but I lift my hat off to men that grow it and keep it. Now spruced up I went into the but-end and went through the normal preparations for a morning cuppa. All set and the kettle beginning to sing I sped out to have a quick look at the stock. There were still two ewes to lamb, one always gets a late ewe or two. These two having sort up (to misconceive) twice at ram time, in my reckoning they had a few days yet before their time, but one is often surprised for we once had a ewe that lambed ten days before her date, so it does happen. I had turned the kye out for good the day before, not that there was much for them forth, but there was less fodder inside. I still had a few "sheaves in noock for the seventh uk" as the old saying goes, for as all Shetland folk know the seventh uk (week) ending on the first day of June old style, 13th in our new calendar is generally a very coarse week indeed. I could see the ewes were all right, I had put them in a small park with the setnings (lambs from last year kept for breeding stock). Next to check on the kye in the park above the house; they looked like typical kye in Shetland at that time of year, lean, lanky and with their old coat looking the worse for wear. They were all busily licking up the miserably short grass; the only consoling thought was that the little they got was at that time of year very high in protein. I said to myself that they could only get better and anyone seeing them again in July would never believe they were the same cattle. In days gone by it was common to have to lift a coo or all the kye in the byre in the month of April, so poor had they become for the lack of nourishment.

The late Laurie Duncan Sinclair had an ox one year that couldn't rise for the opposite reason, he had overfed it. As in Sandness a few years ago we all would vie with one another to see who could get the best ox and the biggest price, that of course didn't pay. Though the late Tony Anderson was always keen to buy the Sandness stock, Edwin Moar the vet was reputed to tell a man that was enquiring into the purchase of a milking coo, "I advise you not to buy one from Sandness or Whalsay, for no normal body could keep up with the class of feeding or care those kye are used to."

Back in the house the milking pail and cloth were collected, I had put on my byre coat, and into the byre I went. Nan, a big Friesian coo with her calf, had been shut in for the night, as this was the animal I was milking that summer, June being dry at the time. The milking did not take long as she was a very easy coo to milk (those folk that are used to hand milking know only too well what a hard job the opposite type of coo is). I poured half the milk into the calf bucket and quickly closed the calf pen door once it had finished, before it could suck and slaver all over me, leaving it the doubtful pleasure of sucking and slavering over the door post.

Jean was now up so we enjoyed our morning cup and our read together. Once this was over we both went out to the byre, taking the prancing, leaping, awkward calf out to a little enclosure I had put up for the purpose. Once installed, we let Nan loose and with a run she was beside her little one, which was by then trying frantically to get its head under Nan but to no avail. We had done the same last year and after two weeks the calf was running with the coo but wasn't being allowed to suck and so was bucket-fed all summer; we were using Nan as our house coo. It would have been better if we had had a calf pen away from the byre altogether, and separated them from birth. We left Nan to her grazing around the area of the calf enclosure.

After shedding my byre coat and picking up some letters I had written, I bid Jean goodbye and set out on this lovely May morn. There was already a little activity underway as I glanced over to Gord from the bend in the road at Milhaugh. Archie Moncrieff was loading building materials into his van for some house job out of Sandness. His father, Peter, was on his way down from Gord to join the gang. Andrew Peterson, their right-hand man, was coming down the Busta road on his way to Gord also.

On arriving at the Post Office I opened the post-box door to retrieve the outgoing mail only to find it was not there. Bertie Jamieson had somehow forgotten to make up the bag for Lerwick. This had happened once before some years ago but not on a fine May morning but a usual winter's morning of wind and snow. Backing the van down to the Jamieson's house, I leisurely got out and fired stones up at the dear man's window, until a sleepy face appeared through the curtains, saw me and signalled he would be down shortly. Back to the Post Office and out of the van to inhale the fine air and listen to the bird song near and far, the wavelets breaking and sparkling on the sandy beach. Far off in the bay the *Milky Way* hauled up the first of the days catch, a multitude of gulls expectantly awaiting their share. At last Bertie appeared, no hurry and certainly no worry, and we gained the inside of the office; I say gained for there were as many locks as one would have expected at Fort Knox.

He began to make up the mail and passed me a copy of *The Scotsman* magazine saying there was a very interesting article on trowy lights seen in Scotland over many years, the same as were seen in Shetland in such abundance in Eshaness, Papa Stour, Sandness and Nesting in the winters of 1912 to 1914. Many of our generation, myself included, have heard first-hand accounts of this strange phenomenon from those who witnessed the eerie and ghostly sight themselves, all giving a descriptive and consistent rendering of their experience. So common had these lights become that little notice was given unto them for they now neither frightened nor harmed. Any and all but the most timid would venture out of doors without any alarm at all, (see my book *The Cycle of Life* pages 141 & 142 for a full account) and they disappeared in 1914 as silently as they had appeared, but supernatural they certainly were. Strangely enough I see these same lights are now being observed and investigated by scientists in the Valley of Hessdalen in central Norway, a very isolated part of that country; no explanation can as yet be given.

Having made up the mail and sealed the bag we chatted for a moment or two and Bertie telephoned Thelma Reid, the now postmistress, asking her to delay the Lerwick mailman for his "Nibs" (me) was somewhat delayed (slept in or something), but was now about to drittle on towards Waas, health and weather permitting. If drittling on to Waas meant rounding each corner on two wheels then I drittled on to Waas. We left the office in a cheerful mood after the locking up procedure had been completed. I said, "I see you fully believe in the total and absolute depravity of man". On this point we were in full agreement.

Off I sped, driving like Jehu of old (11 Kings 9 v 20) "furiously", trusting to catch the outgoing mail van. As I sped recklessly through Melby, narrowly missing one of the Garrick's cats and shattering the tranquillity of the peaceful summer morn, I thought what a fine job this really was, no boss at that time looking over your shoulder, the pleasantness of going amongst the crofting folk of Sandness, all being bound together in a small community with the same intense interest in the land, sea and stock. Sadly a way of life, a culture, which was shortly to change to a great degree with the arrival of the North Sea Oil. Its influx of unken folk (strangers), its vast wealth, and well-paid jobs, all this was about to descend on Shetland as a very mixed blessing, and alter the way and thinking of many.

Of course, this was still in the future and my immediate concern was to get to Waas in one piece. Trundling on past the "Gerdens", one of Mary's hens had a narrow escape as it flew squawking to the safety of the byre on the other side of the road, having been contentedly scratching and pecking for its wormy breakfast on the grass verge. Up past the public hall scattering rabbits left and right, many of the young ones being the result of this year's rampage through the warrens by the amorous bucks. Over the cattle grid at the hill dykes and away from Sandness. It was about here that Peter John Pole was coming home one dark winter's night in the 50's on his "Matchless" motorcycle when he struck a black horse and went flying through the air to land bruised and battered in the drain of the road with his new motorbike drawn neatly up behind him, the forks broken along with other damage. In due course it found its way over to Jimmy-O-Brusta at the Brig-O-Waas, the mechanical genius of the westside of Shetland. Peter had to wait two and a half years before Jimmy at last got round to getting it fixed and then only after Peter made repeated visits to urge Jimmy on. Once finished the bill followed smartly – £29. Peter said he thought to make him wait as long for his money as he had had to wait for his motorcycle, but he paid up right away.

I liked Jimmy-O-Brusta fine, but was always amazed how long it took him to get even the smallest mechanical job completed. If one went with work to him you had to be prepared to stand for two hours while Jimmy spoke and better spoke, bikes and trout fishing were his interest but he was a likeable soul. One of his friends was Curly Jamieson from Sandness. When Curly was getting on in age he owned an old Vespa Scooter on which he visited his friend Jimmy, eight miles away. As Curly's eye sight was by then very bad, he took a large tin of white paint and painted white lines in the middle of the public road on every bend (72 of them) to enable him to navigate the corners between Sandness and Brouster. The lines were anything but straight and certainly not central, but he didn't care. The authorities on finding out it was Curly that had painted their road, gave up for they knew it was pointless taking it further.

I tore on through the hills with the beauty of the scene before me, the summer mist rising from every hollow, the peats on the banks lying out so neatly, outlay and dyke so particularly cast and all drying in the sun, much of it now ready for raising. I did thank God that I wasn't locked away in some office, bank or factory. On past the Girsy loch I hastened, there the little blackheaded gulls were sitting on their nests, they were later to bring out their chicks which would grow almost to flying stage, only to be ripped to ribbons by a pair of bonxies (great skua). It was the only time I knew the blackheaded gulls to nest there. My late brother John and the late Peter-O-Gord were passing when the slaughter was in process. They stopped and shouted, threw stones, but to no avail, the bonxies swam from nest to nest tearing the young gulls to bits. Of course these are the brutes that get all the protection. I know the protection most Shetland folk would like to give them; it would be in the form of a leaden messenger fired from a .22 rifle. The bonxies have devastated colonies of birds without number, tirricks, kittywakes, peerie maa, mallie and numerous smaller species, but it's the usual story, the powers that be think they know better than the local folk. There was always enough bonxies around when the Shetland folk kept their numbers down, a good culling is what is needed and that right now.

With a screech of brakes I announced my arrival at Waas. There was much hilarity on my arrival as at all times there existed in both the Sandness shop and the Waas post office much harmless banter and fun. There then being the type of characters coming in that made for a laugh and merriment including the two Waas postmen, the late Andrew Hughson and Peter Williamson. Andrew was a most cheery and likeable soul, Peter Williamson a somewhat more sober character. Some years after this I had to go to Aberdeen for an operation on my back (disc problems). The old Sister in charge of the

Ward asked me, seeing I came from Shetland, if I knew a man by the name of Andrew Hughson. I answered in the affirmative telling her I had worked with him for years. "Well" she said, "he lay for a year in this ward and never in all my nursing experience did we have a better, more uncomplaining patient than Andrew Hughson." I told her it had been a privilege to work with the dear man.

Once we three had sorted the mail and installed it into our vans, plus *The Shetland Times* for the Sandness shop, we were ready for off. My return to Sandness was of a more leisurely pace, giving time to observe and enjoy all that was around me. As I turned into the main Sandness road a number of Shetland ponies of various colours came trotting up to the Waas junction, some had lately foaled, some were not far from the drop; what a lovely picture they made, two little piebald foals prancing and galloping around the herd, full of the joy of young life. Our own mare Meg had foaled a few days before, on this occasion she gave birth to a little red and white foal. Unfortunately it was a horse foal, but it greatly pleased our bairns and that was the main thing.

As I was passing the burn which runs out of Stanevatstoe I saw a stockduke (mallard) leading her eight or nine young ones down the burn. Thinking she was surely very early hatched I referred to my bird book and found they nest from March to July, so she wasn't so early. I stopped the van for a better look but they all froze at the command of their mother. Not wanting to scatter them I observed the procession from inside the van until she gave the signal to move on again in safety.

The late Andy Johnson from Muckle Roe once told me he saw a stockduke fly down over the park to the voe from the hill. As it passed over him he saw something fall from her back, he marked the place with his eye, walked to the spot and picked up a little duckling from the grass, unharmed. He carried it to where he had seen the duck land in the voe and slipped the peerie (little) ball of fluff into the water, its little piping call was answered by its mother a short distance away with some of her brood around her, and within seconds it was skitting over the water to join the family none the worse for its tumble. So I judged from this, that the stockduke on occasions carries her young from the hill to the voe on her back. We live and learn, I thought.

Once at the Sandness post office I brought in the bundle of *The Shetland Times*, our local weekly paper, coming out on a Friday. As a number of folk were in the office waiting as usual for the *Times*, I promptly got rid of quite a few letters, saving myself a stop here and there during the rest of my delivery.

On I now sped to the Melby pier where John Jamieson was waiting in the Papa mail boat to take the mail, getting his news from the isle and giving him all the same from Sandness and Waas. Off I set again for "Gert" and my breakfast but was waylaid by Maggie-O-Windyhill in a bit of a panic, needing my assistance as one of their ewes had got into difficulties lambing, the head had come but no feet.

By this time of year the late lambs inside their mothers are large with the rush of spring grass. The head of the lamb was greatly swollen and the ewe was small. At that time I always carried a syringe, penicillin, calcium and fairy liquid the latter did in place of lambing oil; as I was often at the right place at the right time to give assistance in this way or that. We laid the ewe on her side, I put off my jacket and rolled up my shirt sleeve, and after pouring plenty of fairy liquid over my hand and as far into the ewe as the neck of the lamb would permit, I now with great difficulty entered my hand between the lamb and the pelvis of the ewe and at last managed to fish up one of the forelegs. It is surprising how quickly ones hand begins to lose its power when tightly trapped inside the ewe in some lambings. Once the leg was outside the ewe, and Maggie had a good grip of the animal, I managed with much slow pressure in the right direction to withdraw the lamb, telling Maggie to had (hold) onto the ewe for I knew that after the tough time the poor brute had had to endure she would be up and off, leaving the source of all her misery to live or die as it pleased. Once I had revived the lamb and brought the nose of the mother to its offspring, she, after a couple of minutes began to lick the then struggling object; holding onto the ewe for a little longer before releasing it and backing away into the house to get cleaned up – all part of the new postal service!

Over the years one gets a lot of interesting difficult lambing cases but usually its just routine difficulties; only legs appear, head lying over to one side or over its back, in this case I find the best way is to tie a line to the individual front feet or foot if there is only one showing, enter the hand and forearm into the ewe, push back the lamb if possible, grip the lower jaw between thumb and forefinger, the finger of course inside the lamb's mouth and draw the head back into the birth position, the jaw is very strong. Meanwhile, as the head is being drawn out, pull the leg by the string back out of the ewe, once head and leg or legs are in the normal birth position, lamb the ewe. If it's a breech birth get someone to hold up the backend of the ewe, this allows it's insides (guts) to fall forward, the tail of the lamb will likely be showing, just enter one hand, push the lamb forward until the back legs of the creature begin to straighten and they can be grasped, withdrawing the lamb backend first. I always swing the lamb around to expel fluid out of its lungs as in the breech position they can drown themselves in the fluid inside the ewe. When doing this keep a good grip of the back legs of the lamb.

With a prolapse, I always wash it well in a weak solution of salt and water, pour on lambing oil, again lift up the backend of the ewe, push back the prolapse and put in a wire clip to stop the ewe forcing it out again. In cases of some swayback lambs, one used to kill the lamb then gut it as this was the only way of delivery; giant lambs were killed and piecemealed inside, but as I am not sure how legal this is now, we shall not give instructions. All this is fine on a beautiful May morning, but not so good out in the open on a black dark night at 2am with rain or snow being driven at you in a gale.

As I left Windyhill I thought little Ruth would have got fed up waiting at the end of Gert road for her daddy to come, but no, the little soul was still standing wearily looking for the van to round the corner. Her little face brightened up and I opened the door of the van and took her upon my knee and let her steer the van up to the house at the same time feeding her on Smarties en-route.

After a hearty breakfast I again set off on my round. Norby was my first port of call and Gordon Walterson was able to inform me of an abundance of piltocks (young saithe), about the Oxnabaa. On to the Garricks where Florence had heard a corn crake the day before, they were then becoming rare, in fact I think their rye grass rig was the very last place I ever heard of, that a nest was found in. Next door Johnnie Fraser was coming out of the byre with the coo on a tether, he took his letter, stuffing it in his dungaree jacket pocket, telling me he had seen our mare Meg with a foal in the hill above Lambton. I thanked him for the information and later lured her through the hill grind (gate) with a sheaf of corn and on down to Gert.

When I came to the "Gerdens" Mary was awaiting my arrival with a hen under her arm, as she often did on a Friday; I just stretched my arm out of the driver's side window, took Miss Cluck by the legs and put two fingers behind the back of the head, a sharp pull and I had relieved her of her life. Turning to Mary's smiling husband Johnny, I said "Do'll no fant (hunger) this helly (weekend) boy". Mary with a flutting hen in one hand and a J. D. Williams catalogue in the other was disappearing into the barn to pluck the hen and gaze at the bargains. The next house was the "West Gerdens" where Peter

John Pole was busy hoeing the yard with his wife Dinnie, fine folk, great workers and they had as usual the best kaleyard in Sandness. Peter wrought on the roads but must have taken a day or two off at that time to finish his voar work. Moving on into Melby delivering a letter here and a parcel there, a bag of yarn to Babie Slater (Babie Garrick), from the Brora Mill in Scotland. In those days one could send down a bag of raw wool to Brora and after about a month a bag of yarn would arrive C.O.D., this was the practice in nearly every house in the country districts of Shetland, for every girl and woman was for ever makkin (knitting). Each time she sat down, out would come the "sock" (garment she was working on), even walking up to the hill she would be knitting away. All the folk were that day most industrious and hardworking.

At last I arrived at the post office, still full of folk, where Bertie Jamieson and Bobby Garrick were busily making up boxes and bags of weekend errands which would be delivered by the shop van later that day. This was a new idea, up until then the shop van went around the parish on a Saturday loaded up with goods, from house to house amidst much merriment, which also prevailed at all times in the shop. As I walked in a man from Aith followed me, Bertie immediately assuring the man, that they (the Sandness folk) had to put up with a postie that had been deported from New Zealand, Bobby vouching for the truth of the story. In fact, Bertie said, he wasn't really deported but literally hounded out of New Zealand and went on to elaborate all the evils that had caused my expulsion, to the fun of us all. I warned Bertie that every idle word has to be given account of one day, and pointed out to the man that little credence can be given to a merchant whose shop motto is "The shop where the customer is NEVER right". Bobby at that moment was making up Maggie-O-Windyhill's box, and sang out "she's wanting a swissroll and you've no brought any from Lerwick". "That's alright," says Bertie, "just send her a toilet roll instead, that will do fine."

So I left them to their fun and in no time had finished my round for another day by 11.30am. Quickly changing into my working gear I drove up to the cattle grid and grind as stated, and was back at Gert just after midday with our mare and foal. Jean was busy with the dinner so I took a hoe and endeavoured to finish hoeing the lower kale yard. Between the two yards, we had about 1200 kale plants set, in fact we could that year have set another yard for both our plantie crubs (stone enclosures for growing young kale plants) were chock-a-block with plants. Though I strove hard to get it finished before Jean called me, there were still three or four rows to do. Inside the house I sat down to a welcome bowl of tattie soup, made of the last of our reestit mutton, and a mug of tea. Out again once our bowls were washed up, there was only Ruth at home, the other bairns being at the school, so the washing up didn't consist of much.

In the corner of the kaleyard I had built a small summerhouse for the bairns when we had first returned from five years in New Zealand. Its size was only 8ft by 6ft; its furniture consisted of two bunks, a small table and resting chair. All this was a great source of pleasure to the bairns; sometimes through the summer two of them would sleep in it. Into this Ruth took her dolls and books while we hoed nearby, and she played. Once we had the kale hoed we moved up to the tattie rig for its first hoeing, it was green with arvi and craatae (chickweed and buttercup weed). I had put a lot of lambhouse muck on it before ploughing. Normally I used the byre muck for the tatties, hence all the arvi. I never knew anyone faster or more thorough at hoeing than Jean. I used to say, "it's the evidence of your Irish peasant blood coming out in you" (her grandfather came from Southern Ireland). The afternoon was warm so the weeds soon wilted.

Soon a tired little girl left the summerhouse and came wandering up to where we were, so we made her a little bed at the foot of the rig with our discarded jacket and coat. There she snuggled down with her dilapidated rag doll and by the time we had hoed our way down the next row she was sound asleep, with the big eyes of her old doll dumbly staring heavenwards. We toiled on until Kathleen and David Andrew drittled home from school, a journey of just over a mile that had taken them just over an hour and a half. Jeffrey Cheyne was with them; I asked them, "why so long to come home"? They had been catching bandies in the Millburn they enthusiastically said. "Where are they?" I asked. "Oh we made a dam and have blocked them in so they can't get out and we'll get more the morn to put in with them." Jeffrey Cheyne was at that time staying next door with his Uncle Andrew and Auntie Joan who were exceedingly kind to him. He was also a great favourite with all at "Gert".

When Christmas came along Jean asked him over for his dinner, we always had a large turkey for the meal, into which was stuffed a cockerel, again into this was stuffed a guinea fowl, finally a rock dove stuffed with a sausage was placed inside the guinea fowl, the lot sewed up and slowly roasted in the Rayburn. Jeffrey's eyes were like saucers when this large turkey appeared on the table, but his wonder knew no bounds when Jean sprett open the rear of the big bird and drew out the cockerel followed likewise with the guinea fowl, dove and sausage. Needless to say we all had a very happy time. Coming back to the events of the day, Floss hearing Kathleen's voice bounded off to meet her as though she had been away a year or more. She was Kitty's (Kathleen's) dog and for that reason she had lived, for she never looked at a sheep until she was two years old. Had she been mine, I would have shot her, for I truly thought she would never be any use. What a blessing she was spared for after she was two years old she began to work and came to be a topper and lived until she was seventeen.

David and Jeffrey cleared off to East Collaster, Jean shouting to Jeffrey to come back with David Andrew for his tea at 6 o'clock and to tell his Auntie Joan where he was going. We sent Kitty to see to her little sister, whom she promptly awoke. The two of them went to play in the summerhouse; as for us, we downed hoes and went in for a cup of tea plus a Blacks water biscuit. Once rested Jean went back to the rig for another half an hour before getting some beremeal, currant, and plain scones baked for tea. I put a tether on Nan as she had left the vicinity of the calf enclosure and was gazing down towards a rig of Shetland oats, now well breered. I took her back, banged in her stake, put a loop in her lug, filled up her now empty pail with water, let out Jip, and she bounded off to play with the girls and Floss in the little house and I to my toil on the rig. Just before tea Kitty came gowlin (crying) up the rig saying David Andrew and Jeffrey had shoved them out of the little house and hit them for nothing, before locking themselves inside and pulling faces at Ruth and her through the windows. "Less-o-less, never du mind my peerie lamb, just du go doon to Mammy with Ruth and say Daddy says his peerie jewel is to get a sweetie". So off she ran; so are the little troubles of bairns I thought.

It was not long before I heard David Andrew shouting down from the skylight window in his bedroom that tea was ready. I lost no time in downing tools and went in for tea. I had killed a two year old Shetland ram earlier that week because I wasn't going to keep it for another year. He had been a tough fellow to buggiflay (to flay off the hide) though I had waited until flowing water (flowing tide), which does indeed help a little, but most rams are tough to flay. He wasn't in too bad a condition as I had given him a grain (a small amount) of feeding all winter along with the sheep, so he just had enough fat about the neers (kidneys) and vail (fat over the intestines) to make his puddings (sheep's mealy and sweet puddings, a Shetland delicacy). These mealy and sweet puddings Jean had been busy cooking the night before. So with fried slices of these, an egg, fresh scones, Voe cherry cake and tea, we all felt well fortified.

Robert had arrived home from the Institute in Lerwick just as we were ready to sit up and Jeffrey was keeping us amused with his tales of "The Rock-eating Galinstine" (whatever that was). Once the meal was ended, Kitty and the boys were for going fishing, Robert having his boat anchored at Busta. I told them they could go but not to go too far off as I would like to go out later on, maybe the back of 8 o'clocks time and try the eela (fishing for piltocks with rods as the boat is slowly rowed along). Warning them that Robert was in charge and there was to be no fooling about in the boat, off they went, their fishing gear still lying in the boat from Tuesday's fishing.

I took a quick look around the stock, catching one of the young lambs with its tail glued down, in a bit of distress, unanchored its tail, relieving its bowel movement and giving its bum a good wiping on the grass. It's seldom one gets a gimmer lamb all stuck up like that. I thought it likely it keeps its tail free by its own water, though I have had an odd gimmer lamb in a like state. By the time I had milked Nan and syed the milk through the cloth, Jean had hoed up one row and half way down another. I took my hoe and hoed up towards her so as to start our fresh rows together and speak of this and that. I said, "if he's a fine day the morn I'll muck the neap rig, plough, harrow and sow the neaps; I think we'll sow the same as last year, yellow tankards, Williamsberg and purple swedes. I don't think there should be any frost around now". Though Tommy Georgeson from Huxter once sowed neaps about this same date and when they breered the frost got them and nearly all of them shot (instead of the swede or neap developing and swelling it shoots up heavenward and doesn't swell out). Jean said, "if that's thy plan it looks like I'll be on this job myself da morn." "Well it looks that way I'm afraid but Robert will give you a hand." That's one job on the croft the bairns hated but it has to be done.

We generally took them off for a run in the van somewhere on a Saturday afternoon even in winter if it was good weather. We would fill a flask and take sandwiches, cakes etc. but it was not going to come off this Saturday I thought. We packed up the hoeing at 8 o'clock hoping the damp would not come down early and help the weeds to grip again. After our cup of tea Jean got Ruth off to bed and I went down to Busta, I could see the bairns a piece off, east of the Muckle Skerrie, so putting my two fingers into my mouth sent a shrill whistle their way. The boat appeared lower in the water than I had expected and once they came into Busta I saw the reason, they had caught an immense catch of mackerel. "Well done bairns, that will do well for feeding the kye in the winter", I said. We soon filled the fish box we had and borrowed some that were lying in the boat's noost there, set them one upon another and set a bag on the top one to stop the gulls getting at them. Off we went out again, this time we headed west for Oxnabaa, once there I took the oars and aandooed (to row slowly) up along the east edge of the baa, heading in a northerly direction. The fish were in great abundance as Gordon had said, dorro and wand (handline and rod) coming up full every few seconds. May piltocks, sillocks and steforns, what a great time we were having.

Soon I called a halt and said we would try for a haddock before we went in. So we made our way out to one of the usual meids (two prominent features ashore to get a cross bearing at sea); I had a spreader and Robert had his dorro. The haddocks were scarce but we got a small codling and a few whiting, "enough in all for dinner the morn", I said. Making a course for Busta we gutted as we went with a great flock of maas in full pursuit. Some of the peerie maas taking the heads of the fish from the bairns hands, others catching the guts in mid air. As we neared Busta we saw a bonxie trying to drown a young scorrie (gull) by holding its head beneath the water, but we were in time to rescue the poor thing, took it aboard and released it once we came in by the head at Busta. We finished gutting our catch aboard, then set about the mackerel. Once all was complete, boat washed, baled out and anchored off, we set off for home, dropping fish at the houses between Busta and Gert, Jeffrey going into his Uncle Andrew and Auntie Joan with his share.

On our arrival home Jean put the big pot on the Trueburn with boiling sea water from the kettle, half filled it with tatties and when that had been boiling for ten minutes put in the piltocks. Once the tatties and fish were done, we sat down to a usual summer supper; what a lovely feed. Later Jean said, "one of those two ewes you have in the lower park has been scraping the ground but she's no got down to lamb yet". By the time the supper was over it needed half an hour to midnight, so the bairns were sent to bed and I went to look to the ewe and the rest of the stock before bed. The ewe had lambed a fine pair of twins, no problems. The kye were all lying contentedly chewing the cud, the six guinea fowl were roosted on the roof of the house, the young lambs laid down along with their drowsy dams, all a picture of peace and tranquillity – da hömin, da simmer dim (the twilight).

We turned in just after midnight. Thinking to myself if he's still good weather on Monday, once I get clear of the post delivery, we'll head straight to the hill, take kindling and peats, soup in a pan, bread, bakers biscuit, cheese, jam, milk, tea and a kettle and get cracking on raising the peats while the hill is so dry. It was a job that for many years before, and since I had had an operation on my back, I could only suffer by raising the peats on my hands and knees; it's a back breaking job at its best, but with slipped discs it was sheer torture, but it has to be done, and being solely dependant on peat for heating, cooking and hot water, the only thing was to grit one's teeth and get the job finished as quickly as possible. Even work like this has its compensations, such as sitting before the fire on a heathery knoll and concluding the meal with a mug of hot tea and gazing at all the beauties of nature around one. The newborn lambs following in the wake of their mothers, the plaintive cry of the curlew and whimbrel, the sweet song of the lark, the kee-kee-kee of the merlin, the hollow pruk-pruk of the corbie (raven), and a multitude of other sounds and voices. The young foals with their multi-coloured mams and aunties trekking through the hill and our own little one, Ruth, making peat houses and pyramids, so were my thoughts on retiring that night. The last words spoken before drifting into an exhausted sleep from my wife was, "I think there is enough fish and tatties to have cold for breakfast". "Fine" I said, "but isn't it a pity posties have to work on Saturdays." So ends the second seasonal day in a Shetland postie's life.

Chapter 3
Hairst

I was once rushed to the Aberdeen hospital by Air Ambulance, being at that time seriously ill, but after a few days I began to recover and was reading my Bible when a very austere man of about 6ft 2ins stood hovering over me with his entourage of followers. This man was the surgeon whom I was under. On seeing me reading my Bible he said in a boisterous way, "perhaps you would like to give us all a sermon". So this is the verse in Jeremiah 8 v 20 that came to mind: "The harvest is past, the summer is ended, and we are not saved."

For this was indeed the fact, or nearly so, as far as the harvest past and summer ended was concerned when I awoke one hairst (harvest) morning. I say "nearly so" for two reasons, first we still had a rig of late sown oats to shair (cut) and a row or two of tatties to take up. Secondly, because I am saved by the sovereign grace and the mighty power of a gracious God alone. As the hymn writer has penned it, "Nothing in my hand I bring, simply to Thy cross I cling, Naked, come to Thee for dress, Helpless look to Thee for grace, Foul, I to the fountain fly, Wash me, Saviour or I die".

I had awoken to a fine morning in late September, it was still dark in the snug little bedroom, through the window to the eastward was the first suggestion of a new day. The morning star "Venus" in all her bright beauty was shining in regal glory. The evening star and the morning star being the same heavenly body, the revolving earth making her appear to travel from south west to south east during the hour of night at that time of year. I was in no hurry to rise, as the clocks were still at British Summertime and ten to six was most of an hour and a half away. So beneath the covers relaxed, warm and at peace with all around and with God above, I considered the day before me. Then came a nagging thought into my mind, did we have enough crops to see us through a long winter. Then came a multitude of questions, would I sell the lambs at the door, or hire someone to take them into the Marts in Lerwick, or ship them to the F.M.C., whether to sell the year old Black Poll ox to Tony Anderson or try and winter him and get a better price in the voar? After considering all this and more, my tranquil state had somewhat diminished, so I arose to the dawning of a new day more than half an hour before I needed to. After splashing a little cold water around the face, and dressing, I sallied forth, intending to do a little work prior to my usual chores before leaving for the post. The first job was to whip off the battery from the post office van, put it on the T.20 Ferguson tractor, start same, by kind courtesy of Her dear Majesty's Royal Mail. Once started, return battery to post van, for as long as one kept the revs on the tractor slightly higher than ticking over, the T.20 will run without a battery. The reason for this heinous crime of borrowing a battery was that I was only just, with a struggle solvent, all summer that year and many others to come, had it not been for the fact I had a very thrifty wife, good with the knitting wires and grafting needles to the mutual benefit of Messrs A. I. Tulloch and us Gert folk, things would have been somewhat worse. Each day that it was unfit for outside work, I lashed at the knitting machine, "a Singer", many hundreds of jumpers and men's cardigans did I make over a period of four years at £1 a garment. Jean constantly grafting up the garments.

8. *The author's eldest son Robert at the croft of Crack.*

When we were first married we had the croft of "Crack" at the other end of Sandness, there was no electric power then in the house and along with the rest of Sandness and most of Shetland, ninety per cent of houses in the country carried all their water from wells. Our own well was about a hundred yards from the house and a hundred and fifty from the byre. This constituted a lot of carrying water for kye and folk. I always carried four two gallon pails of water to the cattle in the byre at each visit to the well. This was achieved by having two short lengths of wood with two nails driven half way into the ends, then with a pail hanging from each end of the wood between the nails I would toil backwards and forwards from byre to the well, until I had satisfied the thirst of six or seven animals; all feeding on dry maet (food) corn and hay. At that time we had a fourteen and half hand pony, "Smokey" by name, an excellent all round beast, for he was a fine riding pony and very handy around the croft, as the first year or so we ploughed all the agricultural land with him. Our eldest child Robert, then eighteen months old would constantly follow the plough walking in the furrow. As the pony came to the end of the rig he would sing out "Wo Mockme", ("Whoe Smokey"), at length he would tire and lie down in the furrow and by the time I came round again with the plough he would be fast asleep, so I would carry him back to the house and into the care of Jean.

We graduated from a riding pony, to a two wheeled tractor called the "Iron Horse", along with plough, cart and implements, so I suppose it was a step up, but one lost the thrill of a full gallop on the back of "Smokey" through the hills of Sandness. One didn't get much thrill in the case of the "Iron Horse", travelling at four miles per hour top speed.

At last we were able to purchase a four-wheeled tractor and I often think what an immense amount of work the little T.20's and grey diesel Ferguson tractors did. Today so little agricultural work is done on the crofts, and in many parts of Shetland the bairns have never seen a rig ploughed or seed sown, yet some folk feel unless they have a big four-wheel drive tractor, Landrover, quad and other gear, they cannot start any crofting activities; often that only amounting to a hundred or two ewes and the shifting of silage bales. What a change here in Shetland over the last fifty years. Reading over this I feel I must be becoming old and critical and shall seek to mend my ways and keep things on a happier note.

Once seated upon my faithful "Iron Workhorse" I lifted the buckrake and fled off to bringing down as many stooks of corn into the yard ready to

9. The Ferguson T.20 with Ruth, in her teens, doing a good job.

10. Taking down a small rig of corn with my sythe.

start hirding, once my compulsory post work was by. Up and down, back and fore until I judged it time to get my cup of tea and some of the morning chores completed. It is a strange thing that if you don't have a watch you learn to tell the time to within a minute or so at any time of the day or night.

I might mention here that the reason the tractor was minus a battery was that earlier in the year I had gone to start the tractor, intending to get some of the voar work started, but she wouldn't start. Thinking it was the battery short of water, I undid the six filler caps and found that the water level was correct, my next thought was that the battery had had it, or that the electricity had somehow leaked out of the thing. To test it I took the starter handle from its place by the gearbox and bridged the two terminals. There was one mighty bang as the battery exploded like a bomb, a spark from the bridged terminals had ignited the gas coming up from the uncapped cells. Fortunately none of the acid exploded into my eyes, though parts of the battery hit me in the hands and face. Once I was somewhat recovered I ran down to the burn and washed all traces of acid from my hands, face and oilskin jacket. My hands were very numbed with the explosion but other than that all was well, but I now was minus a battery for my bit of old tractor (1952 model petrol/paraffin). Thanks to the G.P.O. help was at hand, thus a firm partnership was formed between the post van and the T.20 tractor all that summer. Great care being taken not to repeat the starter handle trick.

I prided myself on being a faithful servant of the G.P.O. and on this somewhat questionable assumption felt that a little leeway and a new interpretation of the rules was justified under extreme circumstances. I can truthfully say that other than carrying sheep, lambs and once a calf, coal, neaps, kale, tatties and folk in the back of Her Majesty's vehicle I stuck tenaciously to all the rules of the book, and after all, we were told to act as good relation officers between the post office and the public. What could a body do when so politely asked, "Would du taak dis lamb (or whatever it was) doon to wir Johnny or Maggie". I might say that later on in my post office experience, Shetland and the NE of Scotland was overseen by a man from the south, that would and did sack postal staff for the slightest misdemeanour, such as leaving the van unlocked while running up to a house twenty yards away, so what he would have thought of my escapades can be best imagined. I believe he was later sacked, and on hearing the glad news, I said to myself true is the verse of Scripture that states, "He that liveth by the sword, shall die by the sword."

Once the tea was drunk and the coo milked I was off on my round again. As I sped through the hill, I thought the hill had taken on a rather bare look now all the peats had been taken home, there to be built with particular skill and care into the neat peat stacks at the sides of the houses all over Shetland. I cannot understand folk now that go to all the trouble of casting, raising, turning and then leaving the peats thus to ruin all winter on the bank. A thing one never saw years ago and its not all Sooth folk that are guilty of this folly.

The denuded peat banks were brightened by the emerging glory of the flowering heather, a sea of beautiful purple. I thought I must get a hive of bees and sup heather honey all winter on my toast, instead of marmalade. (The Faroese are greatly amused at the British custom of having marmalade for breakfast and jam for tea. They say why not jam at breakfast and marmalade at teatime. I can only say to them, it just isn't done). My late twin brother John was the first person to have bee hives in Shetland, he got a fair yield from them but nothing like the yield Angus Nicol gets from his in Lerwick. I suppose there are a lot more flowers in Lerwick than the country, but anyone going in for bee keeping would find it a very interesting and rewarding hobby and apart from an odd sting or two (which are a very great aid to arthritis sufferers and some other ailments), its not hard work nor do they need continuous attention. I learnt this from accompanying a bee keeper friend in New Zealand over a period of three years. He approached his hives in shirt sleeves, his assistant (myself) attired in what one might expect to wear on a visit to Mars, needless to say I never got stung.

Once I had arrived at the Post Office at Waas the usual daily task began, Geordie Johnson had arrived with the mail from Lerwick, he was and still is a very cheery soul, and this despite the fact his working day commenced at about 5am, full of fun and news from the great metropolis, recalling the strange and hilarious characters that once abounded around Lerwick when we were young fellows. Davy Hunter was another driver that came with the mail from Lerwick, he had been a relieving postman in nearly every district on the mainland of Shetland and knew every house on the Westside of these Isles of ours. He would always lend a hand sorting the letters with us, rather than enjoying his half hour break, for which we were always grateful as I was often in a scad to finish and get on with some real work on the croft.

By that time letter writing was beginning to wane, the ugly head of bureaucracy was being seen in every department of life and with it an endless stream of forms, instructions in form filling, notices and goodness knows what, also a swathe of mail shots with every post, along with mountains of worthless samples, questionnaires and worst of all, complicated agricultural forms. All I must say good business for the G.P.O. So good was it that some years later a bonus scheme was brought in, whereby Bertie Moncrieff and myself (on the retirement of Peter Williamson, Andrew having retired some time before), agreed to do the three man round between us, and signed up to a bonus scheme that made us the highest paid posties in the country. This only lasted for a year. The Post office reviewed the situation and got us to agree to a once off settlement of £4000 each for Bertie and myself, then back to usual pay and no bonus. It was good while it lasted and very good on its conclusion.

With letter basket laden I stowed same in the passenger side of my van, filled up the back with the odd parcels, bits and pieces and was off for Sandness. On passing the Gissie loch I saw my first hegri (heron) of the season, I always thought them very doubtful fishers until I watched one from the window of our house at Vatnagert years later wading in the loch of Veltigert. When he did strike his movement was as quick as lightning and his aim was sure, for I saw him down a good fish and within five minutes a further two as he waded slowly around the loch. So I decided he wasn't such a doubtful fisher after all. On another occasion Jean and I were in Peterborough for a few days holiday and were taken for an outing to a large lake; much to our great surprise a hegri landed in the middle of the lake and swam clumsily around only to be joined by another of its kind. They engaged in a fierce fight and then took off from the water and flew away. I never knew a hegri could swim.

As I drove on through the hills between Waas and Sandness, there were great flocks of redwings and fieldfares which is usual at that time of year, having arrived to grace our shores from Scandinavia. Their numbers seem to be on the decline, I understand many are lost while flying over the North Sea (or the German Ocean as it was once called) at night, being attracted to the flame of the oil rigs burn-off "as moths to a candle flame", only to perish in its intense heat. There is of course a general decline in most bird populations, as man plunders the earth's resources, pollutes the air and poisons the environment, wildlife of all kinds never gets the consideration it rightly deserves as man races on, but there will be a halt called one day, not by man, but by God.

First port of call was my breakfast table at Gert; Jean had already undone the kyaar fastenings from the stooks and was busy separating the

11. Jean, the author's wife, making ready sheaves of corn to start building a skroo.

sheaves from the stooks. Standing them around the desses (haystacks) and finished skroos (corn stalks) for a final drying before we built another skroo on my return before dinnertime. Breakfast over I started my lichtsome round, into this house and that with letters and more importantly the news of the place, being greeted with the phrase "ony unkenns" (new or strange news). I stopped for a minute or two with Johnny Fraser as he buggiflayed a hill lamb in his lap as he sat on a restin' chair in the old house. I would likely have spoken longer with Johnny but I had pressing matters at home to attend to, so I pressed on to the Burns to deliver Nan's pills, this medicine business I noted increases year by year and yet the number of folk become less and less in Sandness. I thought, it likely kills them off in the end so I'll try and keep clear of all drugs as long as possible.

Most of the folk were as anxious as I to make as much of the good weather as possible, some riping (harvesting) tatties, others busy on the hairst rig. At the Punds I spoke with Anna and Davy busy finishing a skroo in the yard. Davy was to live to nearly ninety-five years, a fine, interesting, hard working man. Up at Huxter Geordie Coutts was trimming up the side of the stack; a most particular worker. Tommy Georgeson next door was busy finishing off the roof he had tackit (thatched) the day before; everything is very neat around Huxter, Sandness. Tommy Johnson at the third house was busy tarring the roof, "a bit late in the year for tarring Tommy", I shouted up as I went in with the mail. "It will last far better than doing it in June" he said, "for its likely to run off, if it's hot weather", which of course is true, but one cannot always get a warm dry day in October, like the one we were enjoying.

Leaving Huxter I drove on to the other end of Sandness with the last of the letters. At East Collaster Marjory was working in the garden, after finishing riping the last of a good crop of tatties, two cring of lambs (a cring is two lambs on one tether) were contentedly grazing on the green outside the yard dyke. Mimie, Marjory's mother was busy making dinner in the kitchen. The whole parish seemed to be flat out with the last of the hairst work and as old Mansie Cheyne used to say, "there's no peace until the last neap is in the yard." The Mires folk were shairing corn (mowing corn with a sickle or scythe), Jimmy with the scythe and Enga gathering; what a neat job was being made, the older generation were mostly very particular in everything they did.

On I went to the last house, Busta where Bobby had taken a few days off work to get everything clued up for the oncoming storms of winter. He had been to the craigstane at Bunaberry the night before, stating one could have got a göd böddie–o–sillocks at baith Bunaberry and Twattiepund. I told him that if I got through the work on hand he would likely see me, waand in hand, at either craigstane (a known rock where young saithe could be readily caught). He also showed me a string of big piltocks hanging drying on the north gavel of the house, which he had caught a few days earlier at the eela between Busta and the Cornhead, stating there was plenty of fish around at the present. We had salted and dried very few so far this year so I was very interested to get his good news.

The round finished I quickly changed out of my post office gear and put on a pair of old post office breeks, saying to myself that if it wasn't for the post office I would be going around naked. They certainly kept us well supplied with clothing, hence all my working clothes, boots and shoes.

As I was anxious to get the skroo finished before dinner, I forewent the cup of tea, got the tractor started with P.O. van battery, this time leaving it on the tractor. I brought down the last remaining stooks and made a start on the skroo. Jean had gathered some bits of old timber and fencing posts, for the skroo to stand on (I think now how handy wooden pallets would have been for the base of desses and skroos if they had been on the go then). On getting the skroo about three foot high, I scattered a liberal handful of flower of sulphur over the mains (heads) of the sheaves to help deter the mice from destroying the corn. It's very painful when it gets into the eye of man or mouse as everyone that has ever taken in sheaves from a skroo treated in this way knows. After that line of defence against the corn terrorist (the little mice), there was laid in the middle of the skroo a layer of new mown dry

12. Jean taking a breather.

grass, on the completion of each race of sheaves. In winter when taking in the corn to feed the baess (cattle) the grass would be as green as the moment it had been mown, and greatly enjoyed by kye or lambs. Once we had built up our skroo to about five foot I worked from a trap (ladder) till a little higher, then abandoning the ladder worked from the middle of the skroo. Race after race was completed as Jean fired up sheaf after sheaf as fast as I could deal with them. Each race having a layer of green grass over the mains of the sheaves in the centre of the skroo. As we neared the top I took to the ladder again to finish off the top of our bonny big skroo. When the final sheaf was up, Jean passed up the poans (squares of hill turf) to cover the top. Once in place she threw up the kyaar (a type of rope used for tying down skroos) after fastening one end into the lower part of the skroo. I then let down loops of kyaar which were again looped into the lower sheaves of the skroo, this being continued right around the skroo. Once completed, kyaar was wrapped round tightly from bottom to top always working with the sun, until the skroo was well bound. Later heavy fasts (ropes) would be put over the skroo against the

13. The last of the hay being loaded onto the trailer, in preparation to top off a dess in the yard.

violence of the winter storms. We were now finished, and standing back viewed with pleasure the yard, with its upper half full of well grown Shetland kale, row after row of purple green healthy leaves all promising to develop into firm kale-hearts later on. They being of great healthy benefit to man and beast. On the lower half of the yard now stood five big skroos, two desses and a muckle cole (haycock) of ryegrass. The hayhouse had been filled to capacity with ryegrass, the remainder now gracing the yard with a large red net over it. It is indeed a pleasing sight to see the crop gathered in, in excellent order, all lashed down against the tempestuous gales of snow and rain which will shortly commence for the duration of the winter.

We turned from the picturesque scene around us, the mighty Atlantic sparkling in the autumn sunlight, lying like a lamb on this lovely day. How different she would look before the month was out, when she would take on the character of a lion with all its fury and ferocity, throwing its spumes of white spray and green water 100ft into the air, as its merciless breakers batter our iron hard coast line below the house to the northward. From SW to NE ranges of hills, the highest being Sandness Hill, some rolling, some steep, some dark, some aglow with purple heather, the "hill of Busta" standing peculiarly black amongst its sisters but all dominating the immediate skyline; in by from these sentinels of Sandness lie the little crofts, the kye on tethers or loose in small parks (fields), here and there the odd rig of corn going down before the masterly sweep of the mower's scythe, the bent backs of women gathering and tying sheaves, other rigs now bare. The evidence of a "harvest home", the reek lazily drifting in a slightly irregular course skywards from every lum (chimney), its volume being determined by its stoker within the house. So we made our way into the porch and through to the but-end to enjoy our tattie soup, tea and bread. Jean saying she would kirn (churn) directly we had finished our meal.

Rested and refreshed I made my way, scythe in hand, up to the old yard by the sheep house, where I had sown a little square of "Ayr Bounty" oats on the ground that we had had a few rows of "Sharps Express" tatties in the year before. It was rather short, but for a little on the east side; this I reserved for making the dozen or so bands needed for tying up the few sheaves. This was soon mown, gathered, tied and set up in sixes. From here I made my way back to the barn, dragged out the cutting bar and with some difficulty attached it to the tractor. To the back edge of the cutting bar I fixed a hinged length of 6" x 1" timber. From the top edge of this I led a length of thin rope up to the tractor and set off for the remaining rig of late sown Shetland oats. I had found that early sown oats at Gert always filled up with meldie (corn spurrey) so we generally sowed later than the Norby or Melby areas in Sandness which are very sandy and fast growing, as we had experienced when living at "Crack" in Melby. I made my first cut down the rig having pulled up the board behind the cutting bar, the corn built up against the board until there was enough to make a sheaf. I would release the rope I was holding, the board would fall down and the sheaf of corn slide off. Up with the board until another sheaf had gathered (a matter of seconds); one was fully occupied, having to look ahead, steer, watch the board, release and haul the rope as the tractor forged ahead. The T.20's bottom gear was a bit fast for this caper. By the time I had gathered and tied the first row, Jean was out ready to help, saying she had kirned; we just had the old type wooden jumble kirn and got a good lot of butter, kirnmylk (type of soft cheese) and blaand (whey) which she poured into the glass sweetie jar to sour.

We toiled on, each row I cut, then stopped to help Jean gather and tie and in no time we had the little rig by the hay hoose finished. Ruth was fast asleep amongst the sheaves after "helping" mam. Jean set up the sheaves while I took the tractor back to the house, unshackled the cutting bar and hitched on the tattie digger (ground drive, drag type, very old but very effective). I drove up to the last three rows, and spun out the first row. Jean, and Ruth, now awake, came drittling up to the tattie rig followed slower still by a reluctant David and Kathleen just home from the Sandness School, Robert now being in Lerwick having started there at twelve years. I encouragingly shouted to them to hurry or all the tatties would be gathered and the sooner they were up the sooner they could go and play.

We all got cracking, Ruth throwing her tattie or stone whichever came to hand into my pail. By the time we had got up to the tractor, it wouldn't start, I had forgotten to switch over from paraffin to petrol when coming up to the end of the row. I quickly drained off the paraffin from the glass settlement bowl carburettor, switched over to petrol, only to find we were very low on this. Once I had the tractor started, I was switching backwards and forwards from petrol to paraffin in an effort to conserve the petrol, until the engine was hot enough to run on paraffin only. Meanwhile, I sent David Andrew down to the barn to get more bags, then had to send Kathleen down to see what on earth was hindering him. He had found a whole lot of eggs behind the heap of sacks and was carting them back into the nest boxes in the hen house. At last

14. The author and Jean riping tatties at Gert.

they came back up with the sacks and we soon had the rest of the tatties up. We unhitched the tattie digger, thrust in two fencing posts between the lower arms of the three point linkage and put bits of wood across these and piled the bags of tatties on this and made down to the tattie cro (a place for stowing potatoes) in the barn. While I stowed away the tatties Kathleen gathered the eggs out of the nest boxes where David had put them and into the bottom of a kishie (straw basket). David thought he would fool us into believing the dozen hens had laid ten eggs plus the ones they would normally lay when we went next morning into the hen house to gather the daily supply, but Kathleen had come on him and caught him in his fun. David Andrew was delegated child minder to Ruth, while Jean got on with the tea, just the usual Shetland tea, boiled eggs, scones (plain and beremeal) with rhubarb jam, kirn mylk, loaf, cold flesh (lamb) and tea. The bairns drinking fresh milk in place of tea.

Off fled David Andrew to West Coilaster to play with Jeffrey Cheyne, after we had had our read of the scriptures and a word of prayer; Kathleen to help her mother wash the dishes and get some baking done. Kitty (Kathleen) could bake and cook excellently by the time she was ten years old, even at eight she had made a good job of cooking for us all when her mother had to go south to her folk for two weeks. Ruth was in the "backhoose", watching through the glass panel in the seventy egg incubator the latest clutch of eggs (and the last for this year's hatching), the little neb (bill) of the chick breaking through its white prison. This at last giving way after the struggling prisoner is rewarded by half the shell cracking and breaking, allowing the little damp and exhausted chick to tumble out, to lie drying and recovering while its dry, yellow, fluffy friends peck and peer at Ruth through the glass of the old paraffin incubator.

Taking my leave I took my waand (a long bamboo cane fishing rod) and böddie (fish basket) and made my way to the craigstane at Busta, where Bobby-O-Busta was swappin his fleas across the surface of the water. "Any luck Bob?" I cried, making my way to where he was. "Not so far", he said, "but I am going to try a bit more soe" (chewed tattie or limpets sprooted out of the mouth into the sea to attract sillocks to the scene). This he did with good results, for within a few minutes we were both bringing in fish two or three at a time, mostly sillocks but now and then we were hooking an odd piltock. Then as suddenly as they came they took off (stopped taking) and though we swapped away for sometime, we never got another one that night, but we were well pleased for we each had about two or three score (40 to 60). The darkness was quickly settling down over the voe as we climbed up over the rocks to the green above. I said, "The voar night comes creeping ow'r da moss but the hairst night comes galloping on a horse". "How very true that saying is", Bobby commented. We parted and made our separate ways home, it being too dark to gut and clean the fish by the waters edge, that job would have to be done in the barn later. Once home and the fish dealt with, Jean set about frying some of the catch and some were spret and a little salt put on them. These were then put under the gas grill, the two ends of the fish curling up as if alive once the heat got to them, then over onto the other side until they were cooked. I think that is the finest way to eat sillocks I know. The bairns were all seated around the table, hungry and anxious to get started on the meal – fresh fish, loaf, Shetland butter and buttermilk – then off to bed. "A feed fit for a king".

The bairns off to bed and me to the barn to "take off"(to kill) a lamb. I had shut in two lambs in the lambhouse earlier in the day intending to kill one, the other was there just to keep it company in its "condemned cell". Having

15. At the Craigs fishing for sillocks.

16. The author pocking sillocks.

caught and tied the intended victim, I released its friend and carried the hapless creature into the barn, it being totally unaware of its pending doom. Quickly and painlessly dispatching it, with a clean piece of wood I whisked the blood as it flowed into a basin to stop it congealing. This Jean would make into blood puddings along with mealy and sweet puddings the following morning. I always try to kill and buggiflay (to skin a sheep) with flowing water, as most island folk know that the tide has a great effect on the things ashore as well as things afloat. The moon controls the tide and with apparent effortless ease moves millions upon millions of tons of water all around our shores daily. It would be unreasonable to assume its effects are not felt on the land also, I have often found to my cost that to buggiflay a lamb or sheep with ebbing water is a tough job. The older folk would never sow a plantiecrub with an ebbing tide, some would only sow a corn rig with flowing water. Certainly many more sheep take the ram with a growing moon than a waning one and it is impossible to tear poans with the ebb tide, so here rests my case. Once the job was done I carried the carcass into the back house of our dwelling to hang and to be cut down bit by bit as the demand of a hungry household dictated. I always see the carcass of a good Shetland lamb hanging from the hook as a satisfying and pleasing sight, not so our youngest child Ruth, as she was always afraid to pass by the dead lamb on her way to the bathroom, unless one of us went with her.

Back in the barn the skin of the lamb was salted and rolled up in readiness for Andrew Robertson on his weekly rounds with his fish van, he always had his tea with us for many years and bought every skin we had ready. Today there is no market for them. Once this chore was over the puddings of the animal had to be cleaned, normally this job was done in the burn but there being no light left outside, I just emptied their contents into the runnick of the byre and washed them in a pail of water, slopping them into a basin with a little salt in readiness for Jean to fill, sew up and boil. The head was the last job, this entailed sweeing which was carried out by pushing a pointed stick into the nose to form a handle and burning off the wool with the blowtorch, scraping the charred wool and again burning the head until all the wool was gone. Finally scrubbing the head in a pail of water, sawing it into two halves, ready for a delicious delicacy. Sometimes I would gather a few heads storing them in the aeshins (wallhead) of the byre until they were a little sour, only then were they at their very best. A sheep's head is hardly ever eaten now in Shetland, though we still swee and eat them. I notice in the big supermarket S.M.S. in Torshavn, Faroe Islands that they sell at 30 krona each (about £3) and the demand cannot be met, surely an opportunity for someone here in Shetland to make an honest pound.

The seabirds are readily eaten in those blessed isles of the north and on my last visit, a friend Eivind au Reyne, and myself went mallie (fulmar) hunting and took 113 in very dangerous seas at the back of the island of Hesstoy. As the tide was running up against the wind and as that area is notorious for very strong tides and confused sea, it was a somewhat exhilarating experience and a profitable trip mallie wise. On our way back to Torshavn we "lay too" in the lee of Streemoy and dealt with the birds, chopping off the feet and wings at the first joint, spretting (slicing) them down the back and peeling the hide plus fat off in one go, the whole operation taking less than a minute. The mallies are unable to fly when they first leave their nests, tending to drift out and in with the tide, it is in the tide one meets them, never in groups but singly, swimming and feeding. The method for catching them is the use of a long pole with a round net on the end. They are thereby scooped out of the sea and dispatched as you would a hen by drawing the neck, then removing the head and crop, leaving the rest of the operation to a more convenient time on the way home or at the pier. The boats normally used are the traditional Faroese sixmannofar or ottermannfar, twenty-four to twenty-six feet long.

As in Shetland so in Faroe there are millions of mallie and the harvesting of these wild creatures has no effect on the total population, much is the pity we are not allowed to harvest any of the vast number of mallie here. They have in less than a hundred years taken over the cliffs and banks throughout Shetland to the detriment of many of the other seabirds. The mallie along with most seabird are excellent to eat, we have eaten them all, tammie norie (puffin), tystie (black guillemot), lumvee (guillemot), scarf (cormorant) but I must say the mallie is the food of kings. They are pot roasted with a little water in the bottom of an iron pot for an hour then taken out and tatties put into the fat that has come out of the birds, these are then put back on top of the tatties, the lid replaced on the pot and further cooked until the tatties are ready, or they can be cooked without the tatties and just before the birds are cooked, cream and curry powder are added, they are supreme. The Faroese name for them is haafhess, meaning seahorse. When one considers that hundreds of small boats each year take from a hundred to five hundred birds each and it appears to have no effect on the overall population, one only then gets an idea of the vastness of the bird numbers in Faroe. If readers think this is cruel just consider the dreadful conditions factory farmed chickens, ducks, turkeys and other birds are reared in and the way they are slaughtered, to say nothing of pigs and calves. The birds and whales taken in Faroe roam free until the moment of capture and death, as does the average lamb or ox on the croft here, and are slaughtered without stress or fear. Ask yourself the question, which is the more natural and kind way to feed a nation, freedom and death or cruelty and death? Surely the former way is the best, unless we all become vegetarians but I doubt many of us are planning that life style. For further information on the Faroese way of life see my book *The Shetland Faroe Story*.

After the belated night chores of milking and feeding were completed, I set off to bed, to lie and read for an hour or two as I cannot read sitting in a chair, and Jean to her all-over Fair Isle jumper for Jamiesons. In later years it was always six Fair Isle yokes a week for Caldwell & Co. So the house fell silent save for the soft breathing of Ruth in her crib next to the bed and an odd word from David Andrew in his sleep and the constant scratching of a mouse behind the lining in the bedroom. Jean downstairs knew her Shetland postie's day was finished, as she heard the bump of the first volume of Count Leo Tolstoy's *War and Peace* drop from his weary hand onto the floor beside the bed, and his increasing snores echoing through the sleeping home. So ended the third seasonal day in a Shetland postie's life.

Chapter 4
Snugged down for Winter

I did not have the usual urgency to rise that rainy Friday morning in October, I lay wondering if I was going to be ill or was I just becoming a little idle. Lying for a few more moments I then spang (jumped) out and got cracking, despising the thought of illness right away. So now we have come to the fourth season which occupies late autumn and early winter.

A season when the nights are drawing in and the toil and fever of the harvest work is mostly done. I say mostly done for we still had the neaps (turnips) to take up, their shows (leaves, blades) were being fed nightly to the kye, not the best job when the rain was tumbling down and one was cutting the shows as fast as possible in the semi-darkness to satisfy the needs of a byre full of hungry baess. At last several heaps of shows were lying amongst the neaps and barrowing up to the byre began. How eagerly the kye await the arms full of wet shows, they themselves still wet and slightly steaming, having only come in out of the rain half an hour before.

There is, of course, one disadvantage attached to this kind of feeding, for the milk from the coo tastes very strongly of neaps, and in the morning as one is supping up his gruel surrounded with milk, it has a distinct neapie flavour, as does the tea and the butter, but until every neap show has been harvested, this taste must be tolerated. We always tried to keep our kye out until the end of October or even the first week of November, bringing them in at night and slipping them out after breakfast, this being the practice from the middle of October. By that time of the year they were anxious to be in after being only two or three hours out, and spent the most of the day plootshin through the wet toon most despondently, finally congregating at the grind (gate) bröling (bellowing) for all they were worth, until sickened by their senseless clamour I would take pity upon them, open the grind and the byre door and in they would run, often two of the big kye getting stuck in the doorway until some form of order was achieved by my intervention. It was nearly always old Blackie and Pinehoulland that reached the door together both being determined to enter at the same time. Once they were all standing in their own individual stalls, now calm and content I would chain them up and take the wheelbarrow off to the neap rig to bring up their "tea". Since folk mostly gave up carrying everything upon their backs, no implement of agricultural has been more handy or more used than the wheelbarrow upon the croft, whether it was for barrowing peats to the road in the hill, or a hundred jobs about the croft, this humble conveyance has proved invaluable and would need a monument raised in its honour; even in this modern age it is still in use around the place, so let us shout hooray for the invention of the wheel.

The first night we would bring the kye into the byre in the hairst, the darkness would have mostly fallen, the light would be shining out of the brightly lit byre door and the big kye would confidently walk in followed by one or two of the calves, but it was generally a hassle to get the rest of the calves in although they could plainly see their mothers standing peacefully in their stalls. Jean, myself and the bairns would gradually close in around these skreebie (timid) objects until one or two of them were half way in the doorway, still hesitant to go further until one final shove and in they would all at last run, then stand looking in amazement at their surroundings. Once the door was safely shut the sorting out from amongst their mothers would begin, finally the calves would be dragged across the runnick to their stalls where they would tug and wrestle at their neck bands until after half an hour they would resign themselves to being tied up, from then on there would be little fuss.

The day following, the last of the neap shows were harvested, it was a lovely day, and being Saturday and Robert being home we "set on" to go to the olicks (fishing ling), much later Magnie Sinclair-o-Snareness was to introduce us to a very good spot on the eastside of the isles of Burafirth. Robert had built his boat when only a boy using an old done Shetland model with perfect lines, kindly given by Peter Moncrieff here in Sandness. This he patched up and used as a mould using glass fibre and resin. He laid layer after layer over the old Shetland model mould and soon had a very strong fine hull constructed. Once the old boat was riven from the new, he set to work to fit her out with tilfers (floorboards), tafts (seats), kabes (tholepin) and humlibaands (rope attached to the kabe for the oar to go through) etc. In this fine craft we set off for the west side of the Oxna bar and were drawing up very good fish with surprising success, for we didn't expect such an abundance of very fine olicks; some to eat fresh and some to salt and dry. It was to prove a good back end of the year for fish, for Robert, David Andrew and myself were a lot at the fishing in the bay and laid up a good supply for the winter. No deep-freeze then, so it was salted and dried. Earlier that summer we had laid a long line from Busta in Sandness to Snareness, the most of a mile, but disappointedly we had a hoe (dogfish) on nearly every hook, and what a work we had getting clear of them. The boys took two home to try, but I, like them am not keen on what in London was sold as "rock salmon". The only other fish we caught on the long line was a big fluke, we concluded it had been a lot of work for a very small return.

The following week we made a start taking up the neaps, as the rabbits had already acquired a taste for them. We were not too keen to see all our hard work go down the throat of the kyunnen (rabbit), so once the postie job was by, Jean and I got cracking on the yellow tankard neaps first, being an elongated species it is an easy job to pull up, but its food value and lasting quality are not so good. They grow well and we always used them first. Next came the purple swede neap and lastly the Williamsberg swede, a very excellent eating and keeping neap, surely the king of the neap family. After two long days we had them all up lying in heaps along the rig ready for the last crofting job of the season (if there is such a thing as a last job on a croft), that was to hitch up the trailer to the tractor and fire the lot into the trailer and get them emptied into the yard. Once this operation was completed and two long bings of neaps built, we put over them old straw and on top of that we covered the whole lot with möld (earth) to protect them from the frost. Jean having left me to complete this operation while she attended to little Ruth who was by this time totally fed up with this neap game, having ridden up and down in the bumpy trailer until her bum was sore.

A great feeling of satisfaction swept over me as I surveyed the finished job and the yard in general with it. Skroos and desses all snugged down for the winter, the kale looking a perfect picture along the upper half of the yard and between the kale and skroos my just completed labour. So I went in to a warm clean but-end and a well-earned feed.

As Christmas was drawing nigh the volume of letters, cards and parcels daily increased. The last week before Christmas was very snowy, which made the job stretch out way beyond the daylight hours, but the kindly folk of Sandness pressed me to "dip de" (sit down) while they made a cup of tea. I was in no ways averse to this kind of treatment and by that time of day I was on overtime anyway and very weary. So the bannocks and tea along with a news at many of the houses was just a delight. All that week (as in other Christmas weeks) I received gifts of smucks (slippers), socks, ties, cakes, cards with a little money inside, and shortbread, something I never eat, but fine to pass on to those folk that enjoy it; none of us were greatly inclined towards shortbread at Gert.

Once my daily post round and croft work was completed just prior to Christmas, and the bairns were in their beds, I made a start on finishing a doll's house I had been making for Kitty, with opening doors and windows and light fittings which I had sent for from the south, the lights working from a battery, curtains and furniture Jean had completed between makkin (knitting) and housework. It was all duly finished the day before Christmas and had been hidden in our bedroom along with a rocking horse I had made for Ruth. Many little ones and older ones too have ridden that horse besides its owner, all the grandchildren have in their time galloped over the ben room prairie and it is still going strong. So dolls house and rocking horse along with some visits to Lerwick for all the other presents and yule gear, and at last it was all gathered in and it was Christmas again. Kitty was up first at five o'clock. "Had Santa been yet?" I could see that any further sleep was to be abandoned, as she had wakened the two sleepy boys. So I rose, lit the ben room fire and when the room was fine and warm, we let the bairns come down to their full pillowcases of this and that. What happiness and glee when bairns just get presents at Christmas, instead of a present every week. That Christmas day turned out to be a very bad one weather wise. It had been snowing during the night and at nine o'clock it was a flying gale with heavy snowy showers. The hydro pole between us and Collaster was on fire and of course the lights were all out. A heavy gust that shook our stone built house swept down over the toons where Andrew Cheyne had built a fine big hay dess in the hairst. As it struck the dess it seemed to explode despite the fact it was well tied down. One moment the dess was standing, the next it had gone, with hay flying up over the hill before the storm. In the thick of it three hydro electric employees arrived. It was great credit to them on such a Christmas morning, in such conditions, to do their best for us on the east end of Sandness and get us on stream again. After about an hour I went over and invited them in for hot soup which they gladly accepted. Back to their toil they went and soon after we were connected. The rest of the day was spent merrily around a blazing peat fire, with the wind and snow still battering against the old walls of our snug home, the kye contentedly lying chewing the cud after their extra feed which I always gave them at Christmas, and so the happy day ended.

The morning after Christmas was still and calm and once the kye were fed I made my way down to the ebb (foreshore) to see what the waar (seaweed) situation was like, for the mighty Atlantic contributed a lot to the feeding of our sheep, and especially on a day like this when the whole toon was covered with snow and as hard as iron with frost. Our sheep were on their way up as I neared the grind, and the few still below the shoormal (highwater mark) made great speed to clear the beach, they always seem a little frightened and wary when eating waar amongst the ebbstanes. There was a little of fresh waar so I concluded the sheep had had a good feed. Some way off from the shore a draatsi (otter) was swimming and diving, seeking his breakfast. Sitting down I watched him for some time as he came nearer to where I was sitting, suddenly he surfaced with a good sized fluke between his teeth and swam to a nearby skerry, taking the sprickling fish well up from the waters edge, then for the next quarter of an hour he dined on his catch, closely observed by two crows which settled as close as they dare on the same rock. When the draatsi had finished his meal, he took the remains of the fish to the waters edge and slipped them whereupon they sank, he turned, looked at the crows and then disappeared into the still waters. I believe he deliberately deprived the crows of the brucks of the fluke, strange are the ways of nature.

Before we knew it, the old year was done, and on retiring in the early hours of a New Year I said to Jean, "that's a whole year by again in the life of a Shetland crofter postie".

Chapter 5
Change

As the seasons passed and the years went by the bairns began to flee the nest. Firstly David Andrew left at sixteen to go to the fishing with the Faroese men and for five years he fished around Greenland, Iceland and Faroe, finally returning to Shetland to fish around our own shores. He said it seemed easier for Shetland folk to learn to speak Faroese than sooth folk, probably our dialect helped. Three of our children speak it fluently.

Robert also went to Faroe and worked in the shipyard at Torshavn for a while. Kitty followed David Andrew and worked in Klaksvik in the north of Faroe for two or three years. Kitty and Ruth both married Faroese men; Robert a Whalsay lass and David Andrew a lass from the Channel Isles. Sadly she died while coming home to Shetland with the four children in the plane, they thought their mother had fallen asleep, but alas this was not the case. Ruth's husband Leif lost his life in a boat accident that same year leaving two little boys. He was seeking to swim ashore, a distance of a mile to save the lives of his companions, only one of which survived. Though I searched for five weeks for his body I never found him, but as they were both truly the Lord's we have no fear for their souls. Such is life and no one has a lease on it.

One cannot but look back over the radical change Shetland has experienced and the disappearance of its unique culture, which was accelerated by the oil boom and the cessation of the *Earl of Zetland's* trips to the north isles and the establishment of the Holmsgarth terminal. The "north boat" (*St Clair* or *St Magnus*), its coming in and going out at the Victoria pier was all part of Shetland life, as a multitude of folk would gather each night she sailed "just to see the boat off". Something was definitely lost when she no longer docked in the toon.

We have to readily admit that these changes and many others have brought great benefits, but personally I would far prefer Shetland and its culture as it was in the 50s and 60s even with its harder times. This era was brought back very forcibly to me earlier this year while travelling to St Petersburg from Moscow by train, when in the small villages one observed folk (mostly women) toiling away at their bits of rigs, some hoeing, some weeding neaps. How I wished, hoe in hand I was among them, again enjoying their peasant culture which in many respects was not unlike our own.

Not all is lost as we have for some years flown proudly and rightly our own flag, a Scandinavian white cross on a blue background. I was pleased to see the Smyril Line had placed it along with its Scandinavian sisters on the inside of the exit door on the *Nörrona*, all bearing the same Scandinavian cross of various colours.

Change is of course inevitable, it has always been and will always be, it being "an evil wind that doesn't blow some good" and with the threat of the "Euro" looming on the horizon, one wonders whether it will be as big a con a decimalisation was in the 70s.

I enter the following to the readers of this book, of that delightful era when £.s.d. held sway. The articles listed and sold were common on every croft in Shetland, these are the receipts of our displenishing sale when we left "Crack" or "Agnesville" to go for five years to New Zealand. The sale was conducted by the late Willie Peterson in his usual delightful and humorous fashion.

17. Receipts from the author's displenishing sale.

PHONE: LERWICK 69.

SHETLAND MARTS LTD.

Auctioneers and Valuators.

LERWICK.

Date ... 7.12.60 19

for Mr Simmons

Sale Continued

	@	£	s.	d.
Amt. Fwd.		449	11	4
Pans.			9	
Lantern			5	
Musical Box			12	
Vases + Egg Cups			2	6
Roast tins			12	
Butter Dish + Colander			6	
2 T. Cosies + Brass Plaque			2	6
1 Tray milk jugs			5	
Vase, Cooling Tray + Board			3	
1 Roneyclop + Other Books			10	
Books			1	
Hearthrug		1	18	
Mirror			16	
2 Trays			2	6
Pair Canvas Leggings + Shoes			12	
1 Fox + Kerb			9	
D.T.L. Table			16	
Washstand			4	5
1 Organ + Stool			2	15
1 Sideboard			5	
4ft Bed Complete			5	
Sofa			1	14
4 A.R. Chairs	6/-		4	4
2 Tweed Chairs	32/-		3	4
Single Bed			1	10
Book Shelf + Kerb			2	6
1 Washstand			5	
Child's Cot.			5	
4 3/4 Bed.			2	10
9" Mattress				10
Square lino		1	8	
Chest of Drawers		4	10	

PHONE: LERWICK 69.

SHETLAND MARTS LTD.

Auctioneers and Valuators.

LERWICK.

Date ... 7/12/60 19

for Mr Simmons's Sale

Continued

	@	£	s.	d.
Amt. Fwd.		522	15	4
Lino.			18	
Bucket + Bath			4	
Football			15	
Doll Lobby lino			5	
1 Round Table			5	
Card Table			5	
3 Fireside Chairs			4	
Girl's Cycle	4		15	
Boy's Cycle	3		2	6
Chest of Drs.			12	
2 Chairs			4	
20 Peat Bags			5	
2 Clothes Poles			10	
Quality Peats	7		10	
Rapedex Knitting Machine		45		
		584	18	10
Commission £29.8|				
Bar Hire 2.10		31	18	
		552	6	10

PAID

WITH THANKS

-8 DEC 1960

FOR SHETLAND MARTS LTD.

LERWICK

I now come to the section of this book which relates to the activities of a "Crofter Postie" no longer in the vigour of youth, or the ceaseless energy of mature manhood but in the semi-retirement years of a Crofter's life.

Part II

Travels with a retired Crofter Postie

Chapter 6
Unst to Wick

As the short day of January slowly lengthened by a "cock's stride" on the 13th of the month "Auld Nydiy" (old New Year's day), thoughts began to form in my mind regarding another cycling trip in the summer. At this date of the calendar, it always seems to me that there is an awakening, a stirring within one, a realisation that all that is dead around us is about to change, even the dainty little snowdrop bravely blooms amidst the January snow. Its bonny peerie (small) white head bowed in humble submission to whatever weather the good Lord may be pleased to send, heralds the fact that the sun is ever climbing higher in the heavens.

The welcome voice of Mary Blance announcing over Shetland Radio that the first shalder (oyster catcher) has been seen, and the appearance of an odd kokkiloorie (daisy) here and there, if it has been a mild winter tells of better weather on the way. It is all proclaiming that spring is coming soon, notwithstanding the fact that any form of real spring growth is many months away and the cold grip of winter is increasing as the long nights reluctantly relax their greedy grasp on the five or six hours of daylight, true being the saying: "The cold grows stronger as the days grow longer". Nevertheless we have the prospects of better weather to come even when we are in the teeth of a "moorie-cavvie" (violent snow blizzard).

So these were the thoughts that coursed through my mind as I stood by the work bench putting a bit of an edge on my old ripper, intending to rip and flay the peat bank the very first chance that presented itself, as I was anxious to start casting in April (it's a bit risky if there is still frost around) for I wanted to get the peats cast, raised, turned and rooged (setting up in heaps) before setting out on my travels again.

I had two companions keen to come cycling with me, both by the name of Leif (Leif pronounced as in "life"). One was my late son-in-law Leif Einarsson, the other a young man from Torshavn named Leif Av-Reyni, both Faroese, the latter had been working for my eldest son Robert on his croft at

Gert and had been coming with his parents and siblings to stay with us since he was a small boy.

This cycling business has a lot going for it, other than it being a good method of exercise and a cheap means of travel. David Smith and myself on our long journey (approx. 1800 miles) from Bergen to northern Russia, through northern Norway and Lapland in 25 days, and again when I cycled alone from Bergen to Sweden on the coast road (approx. 500 miles in 7 days), I soon realised that one sees so much more from the saddle of a cycle than penned up in a bus or car. Wherever one stopped on a cycle folk would be keen to converse, when we overtook a fellow cyclist or they overtook us, there seemed to be a common bond and interest which kept us cycling alongside each other for many a mile. Also the sense of freedom and achievement, the nearness to nature, the absence of parking worries in town or city, all contribute to making cycling a good thing.

So one fine voar morning in late April 1994, found me casting the third peat on a longish bank in the Sandness hill, this was the 4th day of our annual chore of providing fodder for the Rayburn stove, it having an insatiable appetite for clod and divot, möld (forms of peats) and to say nothing of all the

18. Half way through the annual chore of casting peats.

Agricultural and Income Tax guides, booklets, forms, junk mail, milk cartons, bairns' broken toys and whatever I can stuff into the mouth of the beast for her tastes are as varied as the Shetland weather. Most of the heat from her is in the providing of peat fuel for her, but in return she yields the much needed hot water for the radiators in our cold winters and a plentiful supply of the same for daily use. Besides boiling the flesh, fish, tatties, kettle and whatever the good Lord out of his bounty supplies, its a source of great enjoyment to the many Faroese children that annually grace our humble abode. They open the dampers and stoke up, in a bid to set the lum on fire or, if she had been a ship, produce enough steam for twelve knots. Of course, stoves and peats are things of the past in Faroe, but a great novelty to these dear Scandinavian children.

The first two days had been murderously hard work, having no step on my tushkar. I had toiled on all day until the first peat was out, returning home with a large blister and mortally tired after commencement of manual work again after having had a winter of soft living. The next two days had been little better as the second peat was full of horse flesh (tough stringy fibre), but now I was taking out the third peat and the tushkar was sliding into the moor like a knife into soft butter, no longer was my mind taken up with the labour,

19. Loading the peats.

20. Homeward bound.

sweat and toil of the previous days. I was now enjoying the hill in its spring gaiety with bird and beast full of the joy of life. The larks singing high beyond my vision, the curlew and whimbrel calling their plaintive cry while an out of season young lamb, the result of someone not getting all the wether lambs (ram lambs) out of the scattald (common hill) in the hairst, was now soaking up the warm rays of the morning sun as it lay on a grassy brö, the old ewe feeding close by having a constant eye on her early offspring, other "mountain peckers" heavy with lamb were busy with the same occupation. Years ago when most folk had sheep in the hill, particular attention was paid to get all the ram lambs home early, some to kill, some to "set on" for rams, and they were mostly lambs which had been missed in the June caa when we were cutting all the male lambs, a job the dogs enjoyed, the lamb's loss was immediately the hungry dogs gain. After it was finished I would go to the nearest burn or hole of water to wash my blood splattered face. All this and much of the crofting calendar is a thing of antiquity never to return again.

It was here while in my reverie that an idea was born which would carry me from Unst to the Scilly Isles. As I have stated, at the age of sixty I cycled heavily laden from Bergen (Norway) to Kirkaness on the Russian border, a distance through high mountains of approximately 1800 miles, averaging 65 miles a day in the company of David Smith from Scalloway. The next year, alone, I had cycled from Bergen around southern Norway to the Swedish border; now I felt a compelling desire to cycle through Britain; not that I have ever been a great cyclist, only necessity and poverty had forced me to propel myself along on two wheels. Belonging to a generation that were mostly struggling to make both ends meet, consequently the four wheeled conveyance was a distant dream in my youth, so one was content to travel in style upon a cycle, and that which one learns while young generally follows one into old age.

I put my plan to David Smith, he unfortunately was not available at that time but offered his cycle, which he had had when with me in Norway, to my son-in-law Leif Einarsson, if he wished to go with me. This pleased Leif well and we began to gather a few bits and pieces ready for our peerie jaunt through Britain.

Leif Av-Reyni on hearing of the cycle run expressed a wish to accompany us. Shortly after this a very suitable cycle, in first class condition, was offered for sale in *The Shetland Times* by a Canadian girl. She had intended to cycle throughout Europe but fate had other plans in store for this young woman, for early into her tour of the lands across the Channel she met a Shetland boy and found it easier to fall in love than to pedal through the Swiss Alps, or she may have fallen in love rather than off the bike, or off the bike into love, whatever, she had no further use for it. One fine evening Leif Av-Reyni (in future I shall refer to this Leif as "young Leif" to distinguish him from Leif Einarsson) and myself set out for North Roe and purchased the cycle, which was a very sophisticated affair, the like I had not seen in the UK and must have cost a prince's ransom in Canada or the States. Having paid the asked for price we took the front wheel off, laid down the two back seats of the Citroen and packed in young Leif's purchase, making for Sandness post haste, where we both then tried out this two-wheeled wonder.

Now came the business of gathering together all the necessary bits and pieces for this journey, forcibly stressing the need that we take only the very minimum of clothes, cooking equipment and personal items as I had learnt that bare necessities are more than enough on a cycle, especially when fighting against a headwind up a one in four hill or mountain. I reminded the two Leifs that David Smith and myself had had to send more than half our cycle luggage back to Bergen from Otta only about 200 miles into our first cycling trip, even then we had found ourselves greatly encumbered even with 50% of our burden, the rest safely awaiting collection at the railway station in Bergen.

Despite my one and only lecture, it seemed to have fallen upon deaf ears for the night before we departed, I went over to "Gert", as young Leif was staying with my eldest son Robert, and on the floor of his bedroom which was the ben-end he had more proil gathered for the journey than a body would have needed if emigrating to Outer Mongolia. Having stated that it was a bicycle not an elephant we were travelling on, he condescended to leave three quarters of the assorted array at "Gert", the remainder was more than enough. I departed with a lighter spirit and mutual good feeling, ready now for an enjoyable ride not overloaded. Having sorted things out in Sandness I made my way to Waas where Leif also looked like he was about to carry away everything including the kitchen sink, so here as in Sandness gentle diplomacy gained the day and an hour later found me back at Sandness strapping the tent and sleeping bag, gas stove, one pan and one small kettle to the front and back carriers of my cycle. Spare tyre and tube, a few tools, change of underwear, a suit of light oilskins and a map went into my panniers and that was the lot, other than the light clothing I stood up in, all ready for the following morning.

Friday the 20th of May, 1994 was a fine voar morning and it had been decided that the Shetland part of our trip should be undertaken separately from the main journey, enabling Leif to conserve on the time off Lolly Tait had given him from the fish farm. Friday afternoon and Saturday being thought to be ample to cover the distance from the north part of Unst to Lerwick or Sumburgh, this plan enabled Leif to return to his work until the following Friday, on which day the weekly ferry leaves for Orkney.

Once my daughter Ruth had finished her post round, we hitched up the trailer to their car, put in the three cycles and off we went heading for the commencement of our bike ride. We had booked the car on to the Yell and Unst ferry. The drive up through Shetland was uneventful and I sat with young Leif and two of my grandsons – Magnus and Solbjørn – in the back of the car. Shetland was a carpet of green, some young lambs gambolling around their dams, others in groups running races as the manner of lambs is to do. Every

21 & 22. Leif's children enjoying croft life.

voe lay shimmering under the noon sun, tirricks hovering and diving after sand eels and peerie maas flitting here and there over its surface, as the reek from newly replenished peat fires lazily drifted upwards from homes along their shores.

Sadly gone, to a great extent, was the crofting scene of yesteryear, a beauty not now seen; with the whitewashed crofthouse and adjoining outbuildings with tarred or straw tak roof, a peat stack at the gable of the house, a kaleyard, at this time of year freshly delled and planted, perhaps still a part dess of hay and, if the winter hadn't been too long and harsh, a skroo of corn in the corner of the yard. A red, green or blue coloured cart pulled by a willing black or coloured mare, while folk put out the last of the midden upon the neap rig, often being led by one of the bairns, while an old bowed man and wife forked and spread the muck ready for plough or spade. Likely they would be remembering voars in their young day when this job was done completely manually, with the muck from the kye in an earthen byre, having been flung all winter to the back of the byre, across the runnick until it was high against the back wall, then to be carried out to the rig on the back of the folk, in straw kishies; the labourer wearing a canvas jacket. When the ocean brought in its harvest of waar (seaweed) in April – great brucks of waar three or four feet high – the same laborious job of carrying from shore to rig or to the midden roog, would begin. Often it had to be carried up a very steep gaet (path) from below the bank as was the case at the banks of Gord in Sandness, yes, it was often the old grandfolk that would be working on the rig as the man of the house was likely sailing or not yet back from the whaling; the wife inside tending to the infants hungry needs, along with the housework, washing and making ready the dinner.

Some years the rows of tatties would be just showing, whilst on an adjoining rig the corn would by now be well breered and there would have been an inch or two of rye grass on the rye rig. Lean gaunt Shetland kye tethered here and there would be licking up the short grass with relish after standing six months or more inside. (I remember ours standing one winter from mid October until mid May, never being outside once.) What lovely slick fat animals these would be by July or August. Here or there one would see a coo wrapped up with bags and old coats, this would be a new calved beast; what loving care was paid to all the stock in days long gone.

As we passed through Kergord the little celandines were in profusion under the trees, bluebells and the last of the daffodils were to be seen,

Shetland's only "forest" was bursting into full leaf and with the sun slanting through its foliage it presented a wholly pleasant scene. On we sped through Sandwater onto the Lang Kambs. It was here, just before the First World War when my grandfather John Tulloch was returning late one winters night to Lerwick from Voe, that he saw a ghostly funeral procession cross the road just ahead of him. The moon being full he could plainly see the coffin being carried by those in the front, all appeared and disappeared within the space of a minute or so, the horse was greatly alarmed and tried to back the gig the way from which they had come, it took great pressure to urge the animal past the path the apparition had taken. Once past, the horse bolted and arrived home at King Harald Street bathed in sweat and trembling like a leaf. My grandfather took my grandmother and my mother out to the stable in the yard to view the beast. My mother was a young lass of thirteen at the time and verified all that had been related to me and as my grandfather was a good Christian man I have no reason to disbelieve the account, as there is a dimension of life, and a power whether of God or Satan I know not, that permits things of this sort.

On we travelled to Voe. I always think this place to be amongst the prettiest in Shetland, especially Lower Voe with its waterfall plunging over the steep rocky face on its way down to the often still waters of the voe, the Scandinavian type houses amongst the trees being very in keeping with the old Faroese type buildings at the head of the pier, the bakery, shop and Voe House all adding a certain degree of character and charm to this lovely place. The houses, pretty gardens and crofts further up the road retaining a vestige of old Shetland.

Leaving Voe we pressed on into Dales Lee. The first time I came this way was at the age of seven, I remember being awed at the seeming vastness of the scene before me from about Susetter right on into the distant entrance of the Voe about Fordness. To this day I still get the same impression from whichever end of this beautiful area I approach. Fewer croft houses now and less peat reek but it still retains its charm for me. Passing the branch road on the right leading up to Collafirth where I had taken my aged mother a few years before to see the ruins of the old home where her mother, my granny Mary Robertson, was born. They had had to leave there at the time of the clearances and had gone over in a sixereen to Burravoe, Yell, there to settle, grow and multiply.

What a fine view one gets from the top of the road above Fordness looking out over Lunnaness, Wetherholm and Linga, what a long row it had to be for the men at the head of Dales Voe to the open sea, fully six miles to Fish Holm. We can only conclude by that name fish must have been in abundance at one time. Sweeping down to Mossbank and on to Toft in good time to catch the ferry. As a boy we used to cross over the Yell sound from the pier at Mossbank, the little *Tystie* loaded with folk of every sort, men just back from two, three or more years away at sea, men back from South Georgia, women with burdens in bags, kishies and crates, bairns some barefooted, all happy, all cheery, laughing and joking and of course an odd tourist from Scotland, England or far away parts, not understanding the tongue of the local folk, but seemingly enjoying the happy atmosphere. The *Tystie* had been newly built at David Howarth's yard in Scalloway especially for the Yell service just after the last war.

We all got out of the car to stretch our legs, the better to enjoy the lovely day we were blessed with, soon to go back into the car and onto the ferry, making our way over to Ulsta. The crossing was as still as a millpond, we passed an odd seal or two, tystie, tammynorrie and scarf; the island of Bigga and its ruined houses; Samphrey on our starboard side, once a good fertile crofting island supporting more than one family, now given over to sheep and seabirds as are all the smaller and uninhabited islands around Shetland.

I wondered if the occupants' children went over to school at Ulsta, or perhaps in that day they learnt a little reading, writing and arithmetic at a grandparent's knee before the light of the peat fire and koli lamp of a winter's evening. Like most Shetland children even prior to the last war they would have been very knowledgeable in more natural studies, knowing every bird, insect, plant and flower, having a knowledge of the night heavens, the daily weather patterns and, above all, sea lore.

On through Yell we made our way; I remember walking with my twin brother John and our father just after the war from Ulsta to West Sandwick and being impressed by the number of women on big motorcycles along that dusty gravel road. We were going to stay with friends in West Sandwick, the township my grandfather had been minister in and where my father had spent his early years. One early morning when my grandfather rose he saw whales at the mouth of Ladyvoe, he ran over to the house of an old Greenland whaling man, who quickly alerted others and in a very short time my grandfather and other men were off in the boats caain (driving) the whales into the beach, where they killed and flenched them for their blubber to rend down to oil. The church 300 years before having banned the eating of whale flesh, as they declared the whale an unclean fish not having scales, taking their doctrine from Leviticus chapter 11 verse 10, also Deuteronomy chapter 14 verse 10 – wholly inappropriate as these laws applied to Israel only – they thereby through their ignorance deprived generations of starving folk of much God-sent relief in the form of whale flesh. I believe the three whales taken that day to have been bottle-nose whales.

On our arrival we were soon sitting around an open fire drinking tea and eating beremeal broonies, kirnmylk and rhubarb jam while the old black kettle sang merrily from the crook over the peat fire ready to replenish the teapot. While in West Sandwick I met an old man who had been to the haaf, Greenland whaling and Faroe fishing. That was fifty odd years ago and time, I noticed, had made a great change everywhere in Yell as in most places in Shetland.

Again we were out of the car having a walk around and enjoying the beauty of the day whilst awaiting the ferry to take us from Gutcher to Belmont, so soon we were at Skaw, the most northerly inhabited house in

23. Leaving Skaw, Unst.

Britain. As we were unloading the cycles and saying our goodbyes to Ruth and the boys, the Priest folk came across the bridge from the house to speak and hear what was on. Leif told them we were intending to cycle from their house to Land's End and then to cycle around the Scilly Isles. They thought it a great idea but laughed most heartily when they were informed that I was also intending to go, I think they didn't think I would make Belmont let alone Land's End in Cornwall, little did they know! I promised to send them a card once we had completed our long run, they very kindly asked us to come in and get tea before we started but we had to reluctantly refuse as we wished to try and chance the ferry which would be leaving in an hour's time. They bade us every success and off we went up the very steep hill in bottom gear.

What a glorious view one gets from the top of the hill, looking west over the Ward of Norwick, again N.N.E. one looks out over the Holm of Skaw and a little to the east of the Holm, the North Coos and Lamba Ness (a common name in Shetland and Faroe likely from the fact of the lambs doing well there feeding on the bank's grass). We were soon hurtling down the steep hill at breakneck speed leading into Norwick with young Leif putting his new steed through its paces on this very steep decline, Leif and I hard on his heels. I shudder to think what the result would have been had any of our back-brake cables given way as we were doing about 35 – 40 mph, a bit on the fast side with only two wheels beneath one.

My wife, eldest son Robert and myself had spent a very enjoyable short holiday at Skaw, what a very secluded beautiful spot the house and croft of Skaw occupies, with its little burn in front of the old type croft house, with a garden and brig spanning the clear water of this little burn, seggies (iris) in full bloom, the shalder guarding its nesting site, the call of a curlew in the nearby hill, the gentle stream running down to a fine sandy beach. This is one of those rare timeless spots one still comes across in less accessible areas of Shetland, others being Fethaland, the back of Muckle Roe and the gaet between Busta (Sandness) and West Burrafirth.

On we sped through Norwick, past the RAF Station, now soon to be redundant but so important during the "Cold War", with its early warning system on the top of Saxa Vord. We were led to believe that during the 50s when we had the massive Russian fishing fleet around our shores, that their intelligence units came ashore under cover of darkness and had a good nose around sites like these in Shetland. The cheek of them! It was during the last war that an old wife in an isolated part of Shetland, on rising early one summer's morning and finding no water in the pail to make her cup of tea, made her way down to the well, pail in hand only to find two men filling their four pails. She waited until they had finished, they then moved off to the beach pouring the contents of the pails into a larger container in a rubber dinghy and rowing out to a U-boat lying close to the shore. Within a few minutes the U-boat was moving swiftly out of the voe and into the open sea whereupon she saw it dive out of sight leaving the voe as peaceful as before.

On we pedalled down the narrow road past Britain's most northerly post office and out onto the shore road at Haroldswick. It must have been some sight when King Harald came here in the 10th century with his longships and anchored off the shore in an effort to curtail the activities of the Viking raiders of Shetland from their annual sorties along the Norwegian coast. History relates that he had as many Shetland longships smashed or burnt as he could find and went away well pleased with his effort knowing that peace would again reign along his coastline.

On our way up the road to Hagdale I was impressed with the tremendous amount of outcrop rock on the hillside to our right, I thought great shelter for the stock on a bad night. As it was, there were plenty of sheep and ponies amongst it that day but they needed none of its shelter. There seemed to be a bit of activity at the talc quarry on the top of the hill; I was surprised to see how very deep the quarry is.

We enjoyed the fine run down into Belmont and, wonder of wonders, Ruth was there with the car just boarding the ferry. We joined her, much to her surprise, we had not expected to be in time for that ferry, the journey of fourteen or fifteen miles had taken us just under the hour so we were well pleased. We drank coffee and ate sandwiches which Ruth had taken with her, as we gazed over the Bluemull Sound on our way to Gutcher, with the houses of Cullivoe showing up clearly to the North. Once off the ferry the race was on to try and make the seventeen miles to Ulsta in time to catch the same ferry which Ruth was booked on. The road is a little uphill as one leaves the pier and by the time we had left Gutcher behind, I was beginning to feel my sixty-three years.

In my childhood the only motorised vehicles one met on the narrow mortar roads of Yell were a very occasional van or car and an odd motorcycle generally driven by a wife; the owner, brother, husband or father being far away on the bosom of the ocean. What a difference now, a constant stream of traffic bounding over first-class roads kept us alert and on the correct side of the road, not at all like what David Smith and I experienced in Lapland as we cycled anywhere on the empty main road to the Russian border, never seeing a car for hours on end. Here we were soon tearing along at top speed around the head of Basta Voe, then up the long gradual gradient to the top, then down we sped passing the burn of Kirka Dale, looking east down to the houses of Basta and over to the island of Fetlar.

It is from these banks in Fetlar that the infant child was plucked from the erne's (eagle) nest. The account goes as follows (to the best of my memory). About 200 years ago in Yell a young wife gave birth to a very small premature girl child about the time of the hairst (harvest) and as it was a very busy time of year and very fine weather, the mother wrapped the infant in a hap (shawl), laying it amongst some sheaves on the corn rig and proceeded to shair corn with the rest of the women. As the little one slept, they gradually worked their way further and further from the slumbering child. At last they were a considerable distance from the infant's cosy búl (resting place). A great sea eagle of outstanding size swooped down and in a moment had snatched up the child in its hap and despite the cries of the alarmed women, children and old men (all the younger men being away fishing at the near haaf), the enormous bird winged its flights towards the cliffs of Fetlar. The old men hurried to the shore to make chase across the water, the only boat that wasn't out at the haaf that day was a very old sixareen in poor shape, but necessity dictated that go they must. So while some rowed others owsed (baled) as she was anything but tight, having lain out all summer in the sun; it was all the old men could do to keep her reasonably dry.

Meanwhile, some of the women on the beach knelt down and pleaded before God for the safety of the child, while others sought to comfort the distraught mother. At last the old sixareen with its crew arrived at Fetlar, hauling up their craft they hurried up to a nearby house, where a boy of twelve was busy along with his mother in the yard, whilst a girl of about ten was amusing her younger siblings on an old fiddle. The men told of the awful happening and asked if the boy could direct them to the place the erne had her nest. This he readily agreed to do and thought he would be the best one to attempt the rescue as the ropes the men had brought were of poor quality being the discarded halyards of some of the boats at present at sea.

Reluctantly his mother agreed that Jimmy should help, but before they left for the banks she wisely gave the men a small jar of tar, instructing them to tar her son's feet before he ventured over the cliff. With this and an earnest entreaty from the anxious mother to take great care and with Gúd blessing, they departed. Once above the erne's nest, one of the old men tarred Jimmy's feet and with every fathom of rope tested to the approximate weight of the brave boy they lowered him down. Once the eagle saw the boy descending towards the nest she arose and sought to harass him as he approached her two young, who were half feathered and picking at the hap holding their next meal. Despite the running battle he was waging against the erne and its mate, he reached the nest and lost no time in securing his precious bundle into a bag his mother had insisted he carry around his neck; up came Jimmy with his prize, much to the delight of all at the cliff edge, much praise went up to heaven when on unwrapping the hap they found its whimpering contents none the worse for her ordeal. (No doubt being the first body to fly in Shetland.) On arrival at the house, Jimmy's sister was speedily despatched to the nearby township where the men came and with their help the faithful but failing old craft was temporarily patched and after something to eat they departed for Yell and to a very joyous reunion between mother and child.

Sixteen years passed and Jimmy, a young man of twenty-eight, had the occasion to visit Yell. He called on the folk whose child he had rescued, they were overjoyed to see him and by and by as he drank blaand (whey) and ate beremeal broonies a beautiful young girl came into the house. She was now confronted with her handsome rescuer and needless to say they fell in love and were shortly married, and as Agnes Cumming from Gruting finished telling me the story she said, "I am a direct descendent of the Erne's Child." She being Agnes Cumming, nee Tait, from Yell.

We got just a fleeting glance of Camb on our left as we pedalled as hard as possible downhill and onto the road running along the edge of Mid Yell Voe, passing the haunted house of Windhouse; well might it be the abode of the supernatural if all the stories told of it were true, certainly some were.

The Windhouse and the Setter burns at this point run into the head of Whale Firth, it was once proposed in the last century that a canal should be dug between the head of Whale Firth and Mid Yell Voe, a distance of one mile, to enable the sail fishing boats working on the west side an easy access to the fishing grounds on the east side of the isle, whether or not it was ever commenced I cannot say. There seemed to be no evidence of digging, for I did look as we cycled past. A mile past the Herra turn off to the right is the burn of Bouster out of which many a good sea trout has been taken, by hoovie (similar to a keepnet), or a light and ricker (clip). The house Bouster is about a mile from the main road, and as a young man I was interested in the place, Andrew Robertson being the owner, but he didn't want to assign the croft, his only interest was to get rid of the house, so we failed to make a deal.

By the time we were at West Sandwick I was sure we could not catch the ferry but young Leif urged us on and set a pace which was indeed hard to maintain. By the time we were approaching Ulsta there was half a mile between young Leif and myself; Leif Einarsson being somewhere about the middle. When young Leif saw that the ferry hadn't yet left, he waved frantically to us before disappearing out of sight down the hill, a minute after Leif reached the ferry Leif Einarsson made it and a minute later I was safely aboard, they left immediately. We had covered the seventeen miles in one hour. I greeted the amazed Ruth with "that was good going for an old fellow, don't you think?"

On leaving the ferry at Toft we toiled on to Muckle Roe, via Sullom Voe, Brae and Busta House. As one comes on to Sullom Voe at Garth's Voe, there is the burn of Laxobigging, the word Lax being the old Norse word for salmon, so one can only conclude that in a day gone by many a fine salmon or sea trout was taken from its peaty waters. Of course the Oil Terminal was a hive of activity, and Scatsta airport consequently was becoming busier by the year, hopefully it will take over from Sumburgh airport, then the big problem with fog will be eliminated and a more convenient staging post will be established for the convenience of the whole of Shetland. Of course, with all the technology, machinery and knowledge we have today, Tingwall airport would be ideal but I fear that is too much to hope for.

At length we cycled over the Roe bridge and up to Wilbert and Christabel Johnson's home where a sumptuous meal was soon on the table and after a pleasant hour or so, we three made our way down to the pier where I had a four berth caravan parked, which we used on occasions through the summer months. Once into our sleeping bags and ere we settled down to sleep, I related the account of the two old brothers that lived in the north of Shetland during the last war, on a small croft away from most of the folk around. Willie the oldest, a man of seventy-seven at the time of this event, was the man in charge of the cooking and a bit of housework, such as it was, and the job of bringing in the peats and milking and feeding their ancient Shetland coo. Laurie the youngest brother, a sprightly soul of seventy, was the outside man, having been a crofter all his life, never having slept out of the bed he was born in, unlike Willie who had sailed all his time and cared little for

24. From left: Leif Av-Reyni, the author and Leif Einarrson, about to load up the cycles in Muckle Roe.

crofting. They had at this time an aunt and uncle living in the USA, the land where neither rationing nor real want was known during the stringent war years. Now and then Laurie and Willie would receive a food parcel from their aunt in America, as was normal all over Britain at that time, if folk had relatives in the States. These parcels were eagerly looked forward to by the brothers and made a pleasant change from salt fish and flesh in the winter and fish and tatties all summer; not that their diet would have been any different if there had been no war on, but the tinned fruit, powdered soup, dried apricots, figs and prunes, sweets and chocolate made a welcome change.

When on a sunny voar morning while Laurie was ploughing the "trowie rig" with his two little Shetland mares pulling their small wooden "Oliver" plough, Davy O-Vatnasund, the postman, came slowly up the brae towards the house giving Laurie a wave as he passed, the said Laurie having his hands occupied with reins and plough handles could but acknowledge his greeting with a grin and a nod. Once in the house, Davy flung off his bag and cap and with Willie's "dip dee" (take a seat) sprawled himself upon the resting chair. "Ony unkens (any news) Davy?" At this the carrier of all news good or bad passed on the latest gossip from around the place, while Willie poured them both a cup of well brewed tea plus a newly baked oatcake, klined with fresh butter his niece had sent up with Davy the day before. After a while Davy rose to depart and Willie asked him "was this just a social call?" "Boy its well you spoke for I had forgotten I have a small parcel from thy Auntie Annie in the States, it's not as big as usual, but no doubt you'll be blide (glad) of it."

After Davy had gone Willie opened the contents onto the table, two bars of chocolate, some sweets, tinned pudding and some chicken cubes and a packet containing what Willie took to be powdered soup, this he poured into a pot along with one of these amazing chicken cubes, unheard of on this side of the Atlantic, letting it simmer over the open fire, while he got ready the fish and tatties. At noon Laurie came in hungry and tired. As they supped their soup, Willie said, "this powdered soup saves time but it's not as good as a bowl of tattie soup". Laurie said he thought it tasted fine and he could eat a scabby cat he was so fantin (hungry). The meal over they went out about their different jobs. The following day Davy was up again, this time with a letter from the same aunt and after Davy had drunk two cups of tea and as many broonies, he set off again to finish his round. Willie opened and read his Aunt's letter which stated they should shortly be receiving a small parcel containing the ashes of their dear departed Uncle at the age of ninety-three, and a very few bits and pieces as her grief was such that she had not been able to send the usual amount this time. They were to open the packet of ashes and scatter them around the yard, that was uncle's last dying wish. Willie got no more read than this as the horror of what had been taken for powdered soup dawned upon him. With a cry he fled from the house and down the toon to where Laurie and Davy had been yarning, now looking up at the distressed cries of Willie. "What ails thee Willie?" "What ails me, what ails me, what ails me, why we have eaten Uncle Johnny, that's what ails me". Davy gazing open mouthed at the horror stricken pale face of Willie, and Laurie with his eyes nearly popping out of his head, thought, "I'll have unkens enough to relay around the place this day."

Once he was a safe distance away from the astonished pair he could contain himself no longer but laughed long and loud all the way to the "Little Ness" where the fun was greatly enjoyed, this folk being of a jovial nature. Some houses he had to tell the tale with a great show of sobriety, at others with great mirth and joviality. Meanwhile at the house Laurie found that a small amount of ashes (powdered soup!) were still in the bottom of the packet, these specks of Uncle were solemnly and reverently scattered at the head of the yard where there was a strip of green. Unfortunately a gust of wind at that precise moment carried the precious few ashes away as they were being given their last resting place amongst the cockaloories (daisies), down the yard they flew and deposited themselves among the young kale plants. Laurie seeing the funny side of the whole affair stated, "Looks like we shall be eating him again next winter in the form of a kale heart"!

We turned in, slept well and awoke to a fine sunny morning; once breakfast was over we set off to finish our Shetland jaunt, and the next night slept in our own beds, with the satisfaction of knowing we had the first lap of our bike run over.

Midday on Friday the 20th May, 1994 found the two Leifs, myself and our three cycles safely aboard the *St Magnus* heading for Stromness in Orkney, again it was a glorious day as we left Holmsgarth pier. A few Russian klondykers were anchored in the middle of the Bressay Sound awaiting the herring season, when the Shetland and Scottish boats would again be selling

25. Waiting to go aboard the St Magnus.

their "silver darlings" to the klondykers at around £100 per ton, while we ashore would be paying £1 for 4 herring. In recent years there has been up to a total of 9000 Russian seamen and women on the many klondykers anchored just off Lerwick, so the streets of Lerwick have been crowded with these poor folk from Russia and Eastern Europe. I believe the average wage when the factories aboard these ships were in full production, was around £5 per week. They made constant journeys to the Rovahead dump outside Lerwick to retrieve old washing machines, tyres etc., this speaks for itself.

The businesses in Lerwick undoubtedly benefited when this great fleet descended upon Shetland. Its sheer numbers turned the individual's pitiful spending power into something worth while, when the mass came ashore.

For some years concerned souls, including my wife and myself, worked amongst these dear people, giving them tea, coffee, cakes, biscuits, Bibles (the children's edition being particularly beautiful) and different forms of evangelical literature. We generally found the vast majority very grateful of any help given, a warm hearted, unsophisticated people that had a long history of much suffering. Allan Cowie, a Christian from Aberdeen took it upon himself to learn Russian, no easy task at fifty and was a great help regarding their many problems spiritual and temporal. Also a Dukhobore from Canada, named George Osachoff, stayed with us in Sandness and, Russian being his native tongue, was a blessing to many of them.

The Dukhobore people were pacifists in Russia during the 19th century and because of their views were persecuted by both civil and military authorities. Tolstoy the large-hearted Count being of the same persuasion, persuaded Queen Victoria, in words something like this: "Your gracious majesty, your humble servant Count Leo Tolstoy, pleads for a place of affection in your heart, and asylum in one of your vast domains, for my persecuted people Dukhobores etc. etc". Queen Victoria responded by giving an area of Canada to these poor people, Tolstoy chartering ships at his own expense to transport them to a freedom as yet to them unknown.

Leaving the klondykers we sail out of the "Sooth Mooth" with the impressive cliffs of Bressay and Noss on our port hand, the pleasing scenery of Shetland's south mainland on our starboard, always an interesting and charming sight even to eyes so familiar with it all. That dreaded twenty-five mile stretch of water between Sumburgh Head and the Fair Isle, "Da Roost", that day was at peace. Every Shetlander knows how bad that turbulent maelstrom can be with gale and tide in contest battling it out on a bad winter's night but we passed through it with hardly a roll. The Fair Isle looming up from these treacherous seas and a little astern in all its spring fascination, the high peaks of Foula to the west, Sumburgh Head to the north and North Ronaldsay lying in stark contrast being as flat as a pancake to the south. All this we pleasurably observed while dining on the delicacies Jean had sent with us for our journey.

At 7pm we arrived in Stromness, I always have liked this quaint little town with its extremely narrow streets and variety of shops, hotels and guest houses. Now clear of the ferry we cycled on to the Youth Hostel, luckily obtaining a bed each though it was very full, not having had the wit to book ahead. We set off to find the local chipper; on our way we met my sister-in-law Marion holidaying with the Sanderson family, mutual friends with ourselves. Later we returned, much fortified after our visit to the fish and chip shop. We had a walk around this ancient old town with its well kept homes and walled gardens. At length we wended our way to the hostel. Unfortunately this was to be the last night on earth for an innocent young man going about his own duties as a waiter, for he was murdered in cold blood for no apparent reason. I understand a man came into the hotel where this waiter worked, walked up to the man in the crowded dining room and shot him at point blank range, turned around and walked out. After five years no arrest has ever been made, it seems to me to be amazing that in a small place like Orkney, hemmed in by the sea, the criminal was not apprehended.

All this was completely unknown to us at that time. The next morning broke sunny and bright, we breakfasted, did a few youth hostel chores, loaded up our cycles and made for the P & O ferry office. It had been our intention to cycle to Kirkwall, then continue on down to the most southerly tip of South Ronaldsay and take the small ferry from Burwick to John O'Groats, a distance across the Pentland Firth of about eight miles. Unfortunately if one takes this route, one is penalised by P & O Ferries, for the rules are that if one takes a return ticket from Lerwick to Orkney then on to Scotland, returning from Aberdeen to Lerwick, one has to leave Orkney by the P & O ferry from Stromness to Scrabster. If as we had intended we had taken the private ferry on the alternative route we would have had our return ticket cancelled at Aberdeen and been forced to take a single ticket at considerable extra cost, this we declined to do and obtained a ticket for Scrabster. We noticed a police presence that morning but knowing nothing, did not connect any significance to it. Once aboard we settled down to enjoy a rather bumpy passage across the Firth and in two hours time we were tied up alongside the pier at Scrabster.

A Faroese fishing boat lay near the ferry and we eagerly boarded her intending to avail ourselves of their hospitality and have our lunch aboard, but not a living soul was there though we were below, in the wheelhouse and engine room. The crew must have all gone to Thurso on a shopping spree. We returned to the pier rather deflated and set off for the same town which is only some two miles distance. There we purchased bread, butter, fish and chips, and heated up the kettle for tea and sat in a small park and enjoyed our midday meal.

Thurso is a very delightful small town and as I needed some repairs on my cycle, we had time to look around. Young Leif and myself put our cycles into a small repair shop, where a very enthusiastic clever young man renewed the chain, set of back cogs, brake blocks, adjusted the gear system and only charged me £18, much less for young Leif's cycle which only needed adjustment. I advised Leif Einarsson to put his cycle in as he could not use the seven top gears (21 gear system) and had to cycle much harder to keep up with us. It was only at Carlisle that he consented to have it dealt with. There he had the same job done as I had had but it cost him £40. The cycle dealer was a Jehovah's Witness, what a deluded people the members of that cult are and what a contradictory history they have, as is normal in the cults, Mormons etc.

We left Thurso about 2pm and had a pleasant run to John O'Groats some twenty miles east. Looking at the map Dunnet Head is about three miles further north than John O'Groats, the normal starting or finishing point for all kinds of races through Britain. So perhaps we should have turned left at the village of Dunnet which leads to the said Head of the same name but didn't, keeping to the traditional route of John O'Groats to Land's End. Before arriving in the small village of Dunnet the road runs along the edge of a lovely sandy beach at the head of Dunnet Bay and looks very exposed to the NW gales in winter. Everything along this road appeared neat and tidy. A lot of the cottages whitewashed, the fencing around their gardens was quite unique. It was composed of square slabs of stone about 4ft x 3ft x 1½" thick, the lower portion being well buried into the ground. What a great idea I thought, these fences would last a thousand years and still be good for another thousand at the end of their first term.

As we were taking it easy, we didn't arrive at John O'Groats until 5pm. There is not a lot to see, other than the souvenir shop and when enquiring as to the whereabouts of the youth hostel, were told we had passed it three miles back along the road we had come. We retraced our steps, or perhaps I should say "our pedals" and booked in for one night. There we found another party of cyclists about to set off for Land's End but we never encountered them again on our travels. We enjoyed a very pleasant evening with the occupants of the hostel.

Young Leif and I related an experience we had had to Leif Einarsson concerning my son Robert's ox. Robert had noticed the old black coo running backwards and forwards along the edge of a very steep part of the Kame-of-Gert and on investigation found that her eight month old calf had fallen all the way down and was standing amongst the ebb stanes. We took ropes and went down to the poor beast, no bones had been broken and other than cuts on its head and body it seemed to have survived the fall of about 150ft quite well. It must be said here, that the cliff at that point was not perpendicular, though almost, so the ox must have half fallen half slid down the face.

The big job now was to get the beast back up the cliff. I thought the Coastguard Helicopter would be keen on an exercise like this but they declined. Robert then had an idea that if young Leif and I were to go down and rope the ox to a sledge affair and haul the whole thing to the top of the cliff by the tractor we might get it to safety that way. I had my doubts but we had to try something. The sledge idea didn't work and we had no alternative but to swim the poor creature out to a boat. The waters there are strewn with a mass of boulders, skerries and rocks for more than a hundred yards from the waters edge, I don't say beach for there was none, just boulders and beach stanes. Also there was a heavy swell running.

Robert left us with the ox and went away to the Mires to solicit the help of Johnny-O-Mires, they then went on to Busta, launched the boat and at length appeared some 150 yards off shore. A line with a buoy was floated in from the boat to the shore. This operation was not accomplished at once as the rope got snarled around rocks twice or three times but at last I managed to get a hold of it; at times the swell was so high we were losing sight of the boat from where we were standing at the water's edge. I had meanwhile made a halter and fitted it around the animal's head. To this I attached the newly obtained rope, signalling to Robert and Johnny to keep a good strain on the rope. Young Leif and I pushed the reluctant floundering ox over the boulders in the shallow water then into deeper and deeper water with surf breaking over us both and the ox, until the animal was swimming. Just then, as will always happen, a larger than usual breaker came crashing in on top of us and, had we not managed to grab hold of a pinnacle of outcropped rock, we would have been swept backwards amongst the boulders much to our hurt, as we were by then up to our chests in the sea. Robert saw what was about to occur and hauled hard on the rope while Johnny gave the engine all the revs possible. The ox went out of sight amidst the surf and breaking seas. My biggest fear was that the rope would again get snarled around rocks beneath the surface thereby drowning the ox. We meanwhile scrambled ashore very cold and soaked to the skin, but much relieved to see the ox's head hard up to the boat's gunnel and the boat making for the beach some 500 yards away. Once there they released the animal which then ambled ashore and up to its mother on the side of the Kame; on seeing her calf she gave a bellow and ran down to meet it; once reunited with its mother it lost no time in getting under her and to its overdue milk diet.

Johnny and Robert continued on to Busta with the boat, Leif and I to our climb up the cliff. I was only about one quarter of the way up when the rope

26. Rescue of the ox. The author on his way up.

at the top of the cliff dislodged a large stone which came bouncing and leaping down towards me at a fearful speed. It hit a slab of granite inches from my head and smashed into a thousand pieces. If my head had been six inches to the left it would have finished me there and then. I said to myself, "that's one lesson, always wear a protective hat when working in the banks".

Now back to our cycling trip.

The next morning was Sunday and again promised to be a sunny day as we set off on our journey south towards Wick and our day's destination, Helmsdale. We noticed a number of ruined croft houses, some still retaining vestiges of a straw roofing; I wondered if the older buildings were the remains of the highland clearances of the 19th century. There was also a lot of wasteland which I am sure, had it been in Shetland, would have been put to better use than being neglected and barren.

At Wick we went to the morning meeting at the Gospel Hall and were asked back to the home of one of the members for our dinner, which we did enjoy and had a very happy and hilarious three hours before setting off again amidst the spring sunshine and wayside flora. It was a most delightful run, the first twenty miles being nearly flat, after that a little hilly but nothing compared with my cycling trip through Norway.

Chapter 7
Helmsdale to Chester

At the top of a long climb we stopped to rest and drink a cup of tea from the flask. What a beautiful scene spread itself before us, far to the south we could make out the Moray Firth with white clad Cairngorm mountains behind the coastline, a distance from where we sat of over sixty miles. I don't think I have ever seen the sea so blue as that stretch of water presented it that day. Our next stop was occasioned by our arrival at a remarkable place which I think was called Berriedale. We approached it from the top of a high hill, the descent was a very steep winding road. When half way down Leif, being in the lead stopped, and there far below us in a deep ravine were a few houses on each side of a lagoon, a rough type of suspension bridge linked the two sets of houses and on the seaward side of the lagoon was a high, holm like mass of sheer rock, topped with an abundance of grass and flowers. Ancient remains of fortifications were to be seen on its flat summit. How one would reach that haven of safety in days of yore was a mystery to me. The whole thing would, I think, have become literally a holm when it was a high tide. It must have been the ultimate in safe retreats in time of war. This must be an idyllic place for children, playing in the clear burn or sailing boats in the lagoon, being completely sheltered from the ocean storms eastward by the gaunt barricade seaward, and north and south by the sides of the ravine. The beauty of the place was enhanced by the multitude of seabirds and the flower strewn side of the ravine. It was with great reluctance we moved on down the steep winding road.

We did not make another stop until we arrived at Helmsdale, making our way on to the youth hostel. It was a little primitive but at £3 a night one doesn't expect the Dorchester and we were well satisfied with our quarters. We then cooked a super supper after which we went for a walk around the little town, ending up at a fish and chip shop along with some of our new-found hostel friends. When well fortified with a further meal we all made our way back to our "night's" lodging. It is possible to take the train to Wick from

27. Berriedale.

here, not along the shore but a round-about way through some of the wildest
and most beautiful country in Britain. I promised myself the trip one day but
as yet have not taken it.

The next day was raining. As we set out for Inverness, this increased to
torrential rain and a head wind all the way. A young boy about young Leif's
age accompanied us, glad of a bit of companionship on a very bad day. He left
us for Dingwall at the bridge which carried us over the Cromarty Firth and on
down the A9 to Inverness. Five miles from here we were all so exhausted we
flung down our bikes at the side of the road and lay in our oilskins on the grass
with the rain pouring down; this was not one of the highlights of our little trip!
After some time I unhooked the two pint thermos flask, young Leif took out
a packet of biscuits and we all revived on a mug of hot sweet coffee and
chocolate biscuits. We seldom rested half way up a hill but on this occasion
we had done so. It was with some reluctance that a start was again made,
normally it was our policy to take a break at the top of an incline. Once we
were over the top of the hill we had a good run down but were nearly run
down by a bus which was following a lorry. This passed us throwing up a lot
of spray which must have blocked out the vision of the bus driver, for we were

never nearer to being under the wheels of any vehicle than at that moment. I am sure he never saw any of us as he sped down the hill at 60 mph.

One realises that cycling has its hazards especially on busy roads in poor weather conditions, we always exercise the greatest of caution at all times. As we rode over the Beauly Firth bridge and into Inverness the rain stopped and by the time we were in the city the sun was out, though weak and well to the westward. We pushed our cycles up the hill, passed the castle and onto the rather grand youth hostel. On our way from Helmsdale to Inverness we had passed numerous castles and fortifications in differing states of decay and could only conclude that the differing clans didn't always see eye to eye with each other on occasions. This is likely an under estimation of former troubled times, though some unity amongst the clans was seen at the battle of Culloden on 16th April in 1746 about five miles to the SE of Inverness, the last land battle ever fought on British soil, the results of that battle may have been much different had there not been so many blunders as usual made by those in command. Firstly the Highlanders were lined up for battle on an open moor and, while waiting for the order to charge, the Duke of Cumberland's cannons accounted for about one third of the casualties amongst the Highlanders. When at long last the looked for order came, their numbers were somewhat depleted, over 1000 fell in the first half hour of the battle. If their top commanders had had the wit of a hen between the lot of them they would have engaged the enemy across the other side of the river Nairn, among the tree covered hills where cannons would have been useless, and the highland troops would have been in their own, as it was guerrilla warfare that they excelled in, but as it seems to have been ordained by a higher hand the battle for them was lost and Bonnie Prince Charlie fled like a scared rabbit and ended his days in Italy as a hopeless drunkard. So much for the ambition of so-called great men, ambitions that generally cost a multitude, endless suffering, death and loss as was the case all over the highlands of Scotland for years after the Culloden battle. Starvation, homelessness and a lingering death was the sad lot of men, women and little children. Hangings and deportation as slaves to the plantations of the America's, never again to tread the heather hill, hunt the stag or fish the lochs and mountain streams. It was of course the end of a feudal system which began in the 8th century and was likely the last true feudal system in Europe.

So were my thoughts as we left the castle behind and entered the hostel which looked as if it had been some great house in its day. On the next day, much refreshed we set off on our ever decreasing journey but not before we had gathered together so much unnecessary luggage, which we got rid of at the post office. This lightened our cycles considerably. We at last had but the bare necessities with us, the rest was on its way to Shetland. Firstly, we travelled within sight of the River Ness canal which opened up to receive the waters of Loch Ness along whose edge we cycled on that lovely spring day, ever keeping an eye open for its monster as we bounded along at a steady 15mph. Yachts and sailboats added to the beauty of the scene, the mountains with their wooded slopes made an impressive picture. Leif Einarsson stopped at every vantage point to gaze and photograph. Young Leif, having travelled extensively through Scandinavia and Europe was somewhat less taken with the surroundings, though enjoying this part of our trip.

We stopped at an old castle where a lone piper was playing a lament, the fee for entry to the castle was £3 per person, and as the boys were not interested we just pressed on. Coming to a roadside hotel we noticed a strange craft tied up alongside the hotel's small jetty. On inspection, we found it was some kind of submarine whereupon the two Leifs were very keen to take a trip in it, until they were informed of the price – £68 per person. The way it appeared to operate was that a motor boat towed the thing through the loch, and once it was ready to submerge the two side fins were directed downwards and the craft descended into the murky depths and as we could see no search light upon the craft, our conclusion was you would see very little for your £68. Perhaps they employed a tame Loch Ness Monster to scare the passengers half a league beneath the waves; what will some folk do to wheedle money out of tourists.

The pleasant run of thirty-two miles ended at the NE end of the Caledonian canal which is sixty miles long but only twenty-two miles actual canal, the rest being made up of the lochs it connects. Starting with Loch Linnhe and ending in the Moray Firth, it was completed in about 1845 and has about thirty locks. We arrived at Fort Augustus where a very smart converted sea barge was in the lock, being floated up to the canal level which was somewhat higher than Loch Ness. Here we, like the man in Luke's gospel 16 v 19, dined 'sumptuously', as the run from Inverness had quickened in us a hearty appetite. All manner of people besides tourists had gathered, Highland tinkers played on their ancient pipes, food vendors, ice cream vans and souvenir-sellers all seemed to congregate around the end of the canal in a bid to extract something from someone but had no luck with us. Clouds began to

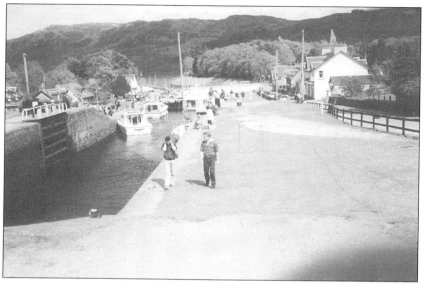

28. Caledonian canal.

drift in from the SW and we concluded we had enjoyed the best of that day, which proved to be the case by 4pm. Meanwhile we washed and packed up our pots and pans and set off again.

After having travelled only half a mile we stopped to look at a large model of "Nessie" the monster. There a well meaning man persuaded us to go back to the head of the loch and travel to Aberchalder not by the road but by the towpath on the edge of the canal assuring us that the path surface was very good and that we would cut off a mile and a half. So back we went and onto the towpath and found the first half-mile as we had been told but after that, one could only describe it as being atrocious. How we didn't get a puncture or buckled wheel I don't know. We were reduced to walking speed, it may have been slightly shorter but it took us an hour longer to complete the journey. At length we joined the main road at the head of Loch Oich which led onto Loch Lochy. There we found a youth hostel, just as the heavens opened and down came the rain in torrents. What a friendly bunch of hostellers were gathered there including five lawyers; they were cycling from Land's End to John O'Groats. Here Leif Einarsson and myself were to get help for the inside of our upper limbs as they were chaffed raw from our cycling and were bleeding quite a bit. One on the lawyers had suffered the same distress and found that foot powder was the answer, this he supplied and after we had purchased a wide roll of cotton wool and padded the affected area, it healed up after about a week but right to the end of our trip we applied the powder and had no more trouble.

That night I related to the two Leifs the true event of a burial at Sandness. It so happened that the folk on the north side of the burn at Dale of Walls are buried in Sandness, some three miles over the hills, and on this occasion an elderly person died on the north side of the burn in Dale. Word was then sent to the grave digger in Sandness and the minister in Watsness informing them that the funeral would take place at such and such a time two days hence. They were to send men around Sandness to bid the men of the place to attend the burial. When the time came around all the Sandness men arrived at the kirkyard but neither coffin nor Dale men showed up and after waiting for over an hour, four Sandness men set off over Sandness hill to see what was delaying the funeral. A mile into their journey they found a Dale man lying paralytic on his back in the heather. A little further on another of the pallbearers in the same state until all eight men were found in the hills the worse for drink. After some search the coffin was found lying in a burn, this the Sandness men carried onto its last resting place in the Sandness Kirkyard minus the pallbearers. Of course, this happened many years ago.

Once my tale was told we turned in and enjoyed seven hours of sound sleep. I awoke just before ten to five the next morning and lay listening to the wind and heavy rain on the window of the dormitory. While the other members of the room were blissfully oblivious to the day ahead of us, I thought it was lucky for some, for our lawyer friends would flee before the gale and rain on their journey NE along the lochs to Inverness, almost effortlessly, while we would have to struggle every yard of the way to Fort William and probably further. I rose and washed, thinking what a useless exercise on a morning like this, for we would be well washed shortly. By the time I was half dressed Leif Einarsson was up, and as usual his cheery indomitable self. I never ever met a man so unaffected by any form of hardship or disaster as Leif, and felt honoured to have had him as a son-in-law. Giving me his morning greeting, "how are you auld Daa?" Leif then stirred our young friend, who would have quickly turned over and slept on when he heard the rain lashing on the window pane, but we insisted on his rising. We breakfasted on porridge, bacon and tomatoes and eggs (three each), toast and marmalade. I left the two Leifs to wash up and pack while I swept out the dormitory; one is obliged to do some form of work at a youth hostel.

Later, clad in our oilskins we struggled off in a SW direction, thinking what a wet airt the SW is. The Highlands of Scotland seem to get more than their fair share of water from that direction, making it a very doubtful place for a sunny holiday. Many of its people believe that the Forestry Commission is answerable for at least 50% of the wet, by filling every glen and mountainside with pine trees; they claim the trees cause the rain. Having myself worked for two years in the forestry in Argyll as a gamekeeper and then as a horseman, it did seem to rain ceaselessly, but whether or not the Commission is to blame I cannot say, but all trees and plant life take in carbon dioxide and give off oxygen, so trees in great numbers maybe do cause a bigger rain fall.

Leif Einarsson, as was his habit in adverse weather conditions, took the lead to give me a little shelter and in turn young Leif followed me, each keeping not more than six inches behind the back wheel of the cyclist in front and so getting a little lee from Leif Einarsson.

The journey from the hostel to Fort William is only twenty-five miles but took us four hours of very hard slogging; we determined just to keep going and have a good rest once there. We met two young lasses hitch hiking, they were very wet, tired and miserable and going our way into the face of the weather and were very unlikely to get a lift in a car in their state. I thought perhaps a van would pick them up. Once into the town we lost no time in finding a warm café and sat there for an hour, being fortified with hot Scotch broth, a bacon roll and coffee, we felt more able for the afternoon and evening's bike ride. On leaving the café we found to our great delight our giant enemy the wind had gone to sleep and the rain was beginning to abate.

After a look around the town, wonder of wonders the clouds rolled away and out came the sun and there in all its majestic glory stood Ben Nevis some five miles to the eastward; because of its great height (4406 feet) it appeared much nearer. As we had no intention of scaling its giddy heights, though every other shop seemed to cater for that sport, we made our way out of town on our fifty mile jaunt to Oban. This could have been shortened by five miles if we had paid more attention to a friendly soul we met while stopping for our tea break at the side of the road. This dear man told us that at Creagan inn there is an old unused bridge spanning Loch Creran which walkers and cyclists use to their advantage, for it saves one the long journey around the head of the loch. We, being so dazzled by the beauty of our surroundings, never saw the bridge until we cycled past it on our way up the other side of the loch.

The run from Fort William to Oban in good weather is indeed very impressive, with its high mountains and wild moorland on one side and the beauty of the blue waters of Loch Linnhe on the other. We rolled into Oban at 6pm, again making for the youth hostel to secure a bed before doing anything else. Once installed we put our cycles in the now very crowded cycle shed, our gear on the respective beds and out into the town which was crowded with holiday-makers, in the form of cyclists, hikers, hotel residents, walkers and talkers. I had been twice before to this town, once with a girl friend some forty-one years before and again thirty-nine years previously with my twin brother, to buy a horse. The town was full of vendors of every kind, everyone and everything geared up for the tourist industry.

How different I found the place from my first visit, I liked it better then of course, being young and having a pretty girl with me it was bound to make a difference. We had come to Scotland on a 500cc BSA motorbike, touring through the Highlands. The weather then being very mixed, but we didn't seem to notice it, just enjoying the wonder of the lochs, mountains, forest, rivers and our own company. Of course, at that time I was a Godless worldly young person but within three years a most radical, remarkable and wondrous change took place in my life when I was awakened to my true position as a sinner, by the inward working of God's Holy Spirit within my innermost being. When six months later God translated me from a state of spiritual darkness into divine light, from spiritual death unto abundant life, from the doldrums of sin into the forgiveness, liberty and peace of God, outside any labour or human merit, a work of sovereign grace had taken place within my soul and I became a new creature in Christ Jesus (2 Corinthians 5 verse 17). What did I do? nothing, God did it all; I believed to the eternal saving of my soul, for salvation is of the Lord and of Him alone.

As Oban is one of the ferry ports to the isles, the hostel was the departure and arrival point for the youth of every nation, leaving for and returning from South Uist, Colonsay, Mull, Lismore Island, Coll and Tiree. As we made our way along the seafront to the nearest "chipper" we observed a large building on the skyline overlooking the town. Young Leif at once wished to know what it was. I told him it was McCaig's "folly", an unfinished replica of the Roman Colosseum, commenced in 1897 by a banker by the name of McCaig and I said that the ruined castle we saw was built in the 13th century and was called Dunollie Castle. "How do you know all this for we have just arrived?" he asked. I then had to tell him that I had been here twice before; he was much less impressed by his guide. We found the fish and chip shop but they were rather mean with the amount of chips and the fish was not as fresh as in Shetland but we enjoyed it just the same as we made our way back to the cheery throng in the hostel.

After a sound sleep and a hearty breakfast we set off amidst sunshine and bird song along the A816 with all its wild beauty. From Oban to Loch Melfort then on to Loch Craignish with its many holms. This was the most beautiful area of Scotland so far, the wooded parts carpeted with bluebells, the sides of the road with celandines and primroses and amongst the trees we saw several red deer. We left this very picturesque scene to head inland and upward from Kintraw. It seemed like it was uphill all the way until one runs down to Lochgilphead. Although we found it a very hard climb there were compensations along the way, for at Kilmartin there are a mass of prehistoric sites of much interest. What castles, forts, earthworks, broch's, burial mounds and standing stones there were on our route from Thurso to the south. One would think the ancients expelled all their energies building and fighting. Of course the Clan history is full of battles, mostly over stolen cattle, insulted chiefs, peerie bits of land and hatred for each other, little peace just warfare and sorrow.

We arrived at Lochgilphead but carried onto Tarbet feeling disjaskit (exhausted), or should I say young Leif and I were, nothing seemed to weary Leif Einarsson. Oh to be as strong as him, for while we were exhausted, off he went to one of the shops along the waterfront while we two tired souls sat on a bench overlooking the sea loch. Shortly after, Leif arrived back with a large punnet of strawberries for each of us plus a carton of double cream. (We had to baptise the strawberries in the cream as the punnets had holes in them.) After consuming these we were somewhat revived and while the two Leifs got the soup and kettle heated, I went over to a shop and bought hot pies, chips and rolls. There we sat, ate, spoke and laughed until it was time to leave this quaint quiet little backwater on Loch Fyne amidst the mountains and lochs. We cycled about seven miles along the A83 until we came to Whitehouse and turned to the left onto the B8001; for the next seven miles we sweated and toiled over a series of very steep mountains, until we arrived at a jetty, only to see the ferry had just left three minutes before we arrived. The terminal boasted a waiting room, telephone box and timetables which told us we had another hour to wait for the next ferry and as it had become very cold and wet we went into the waiting room and drank a cup of coffee from the flask and lay down on the seats, not to sleep but to doze and speak to the two little girls that ran around, happily unconcerned whether it was an hour or a day or a week until the ferry came back. Their parents were schoolteachers from somewhere in England. They kindly offered to take our cycles in their mobile home to the top of the very steep pass on the Island of Arran (Glen Chalmadale). We thanked them but said we thought it would be cheating. At last the ferry was back and after it had spewed out a line of cars from its belly, we along with our new-found friends embarked for our journey across Kilbrannan Sound for the Island of Arran. By the time we landed, the rain had gone and it had become a very warm afternoon.

Arran is indeed a most lovely island and well worth a visit. We landed at Lochranza on the NW corner of the Isle and as we still had fourteen miles to go until we were at Brodick, where we intended to stay the night, we did not delay. As we were passing the camping site at the commencement of our climb, a girl of about fifteen stopped us, weeping and appealing for our help, as a dog she had been left in charge of had escaped and was running full bore down the road. The dog would get into trouble, she cried, and she would get into even worse trouble, she told us, but all our efforts were in vain, so we had at last to leave the girl to her fate. I told young Leif I thought she would likely escape the gallows but incur forty lashes for her stupidity, poor lass.

We had to walk pushing our bikes for the next hour, until we had at last made the top of the pass; what a climb on a hot early evening. Halfway up this mountain road we found an adder that had been run over. I was very surprised as I had no idea snakes lived in Scotland. One connects them more with the warmer climes of merry England, but adder it was and dead it was, poor thing. Once on the descent we hurtled down at a tremendous rate of knots, through the beautiful wooded terrain, until at last we were at sea level and the warm sunshine gave way to heavy rain and a head wind. At length we made Brodick and after a search found the tourist information office which to our relief was still open. They with much difficulty found us a B & B at £13 each, so we parked our cycles in the proprietor's garage, signed the book and made for the nearest chipper. The two Leifs had chicken and chips, I had blood pudding and chips. After our feed we made our way back to our place of abode and as there was plenty of tea, coffee and milk in our bedroom, we took up some of our "Board of Trade Rations" from the saddlebags on our cycles and had another good feed before turning in, wondering how the weeping maiden had fared over her misanter (mishap) concerning the hound.

This brought to my mind a true story told to me in Faroe, so I related it to my young companions. It so happened that in the 1930s in the longest village in Faroe, Kollafjörd, that a large family was having a struggle to make ends meet; the bairns were all young, the father had little work, the mother had a constant worry trying to keep them all fed, but added to their burden was the unwelcome visit each day at dinner time of the local layabout. When the frugal meal was on the table he would sit up with them and make sure he got his good share. This went on for some weeks until the man of the house had had enough. Just at that time their aged hound died, the husband had an idea to get rid of this "bum" so he told his wife to make their dinner an hour earlier than usual. In the meanwhile he took the smelly old dog below the house into the byre, skinned it and boiled it in an old pot outside. When at length it was cooked he carried it up into the house and set up a place on the empty table for their "visitor". He at length came in and wanted to know why they had dined early, he was told they were going to walk the ten miles into Torshavn. So the man sat down and got stuck into the plate of "stew", complaining that the meat was very tough but quite tasty. Once finished he lay back in his chair and enquired where his old friend the dog was today, for he always made a fuss of it. The husband then flung the skin of the old hound at his feet saying, "that's its hide and you have eaten its flesh". Needless to say they never had a visit from the layabout again. The Leifs enjoyed the story stating it made them feel rather hungry, but as there were no dogs around, we went to sleep.

We awoke the next morning to a day of distress, wind and rain, one doesn't mind these elements when they are acting in one's favour, but one look outside through the rain bespattered window to the sea beyond told it all. Strong wind and rain from the south'ard, which offered no favours but bespoke hard labour and discomfort. I am sure that had it been a "blinnd moorie" (a severe snowstorm where nothing can be seen), Leif Einarsson would have been just as happy, nothing ever seemed to depress his buoyant spirit. We went downstairs to enjoy the breakfast part of the B & B, as usual the cereals were in small packets of differing kinds from Alpen to Shredded Wheat. I think it is expected of the boarders that they select one packet of their favourite choice. Young Leif always selected four or five packets of his favourite choice, bidding the landlady to replenish the large milk jug every now and again. It just goes to show how very different bed & breakfast establishments are in Scandinavia. Leif Einarsson and I had guiltily taken two packets, furtively hiding our second one until our first was eaten. Young Leif openly scoffed the lot while holding a pleasant conversation with the aghast landlady. Once we had downed our cereal we ordered a full English breakfast along with toast and marmalade. Young Leif asked for refills of the toast rack and marmalade dish. I think the dear woman was glad to see us go and did not ask us back or give us her card.

We headed for the early ferry which left immediately we boarded. We calculated we were only just one up on the last ferry which took us to Arran, having missed it by a hair's breadth. The trip over to Ardrossan was uneventful and took about an hour. On our arrival we just followed the line of traffic to the main road, seeing no-one on foot, partly because of the blinding rain, the other reason being there was no-one. We turned right which was as far as we could guess in WSW direction, hoping to see a sign for Kilmarnock. We saw nothing other than fast moving congested traffic, roundabouts and flyovers. When all hope was about gone, we, or rather Leif Einarsson, saw a sign to Kilmarnock, so we battled on. The main road skirts the town for which we were glad as we had no desire to visit the town. The only connection I have had with the town is that John Ritchie's book printing and selling establishment resides there and as I feel the price of their Christian books are grossly inflated, I shop elsewhere!

Taking the A76 we headed for Mauchline; as we neared it we had a very long hill to add to our difficulties. At its summit there was a very third rate café into which we filed like three drowned rats. Shedding our oilskins we flopped into a chair each and ordered tea, coffee and drinking chocolate and cream cakes. Never was anything more appreciated for we were just done in and had only covered twenty miles. I thought we'd be lucky to get forty miles of our journey at this speed today. Young Leif drew out a £10 note from his inside pocket, which my next door neighbour Marjory Fraser had given him just before we left, telling him to buy us all a cup of tea on the road. We settled down to spend this aamos (gift) on more mugs of the same, plus cream cakes, until we had spent it all and headed out after an hours rest much revived and fortified for the road ahead. We pedalled on for the next twelve miles to New Cumnock and low and behold the weather changed completely, the sun came out in all its brilliance, the wind went away to the NW and we were bounding along at 20mph through hilly attractive scenery which literally seethed with rabbits. Never had we seen so many "kyunnen" and quite tame. I thought the foxes and whitraat (stoat) wouldn't go hungry hereabouts. The abundance of flora, broad-leafed trees and bird life seemed to complete the beauty of our pleasant surroundings.

By the time we reached the outskirts of Dumfries at 7pm, having covered seventy-five miles, I was all in and thought we should look for a youth hostel for the night, but the two Leifs urged me to keep going and try and make my youngest son's place the other side of Carlisle. There was just one mug of coffee left in the flask. This they gave me along with some biscuits while I sat propped up against a farm gate, and after half an hour, I felt a bit better and we set off again. I was so tired I couldn't think; I just kept turning the pedals until at last we came to Gretna Green. Here we made a foolish mistake in thinking the dual carriageway was a motorway into Carlisle, and instead of taking it we sought another route via Langtown, after which we got lost and by the time we got into Carlisle it was midnight. Leif Einarsson had no lights so we kept him in the middle of our convoy and prayed the police weren't around. Once in the centre of Carlisle we only had four miles to go to the village of Scotby, where my now dear departed daughter-in-law Liz was waiting up to welcome us, as we had phoned her from Gretna Green. Young Leif and I were very worn out and I lay in a hot bath with a mug of tea and a slice of hot toast oozing with butter. We had covered 122 miles and I felt my sixty-three years as I lay there. It would only have been 116 miles if we had had a little wit and kept to the main road. My son David Andrew was at sea and my grandchildren safely asleep, so at about 1.30am we bade Liz "good morning" and went down into the lower garden where I kept my caravan and were soon sound asleep.

We slept on until 9am and after breakfast set off for Carlisle to get Leif Einarsson's cycle fixed. I like this small northern city with its ancient castle on the banks of the river Eden; an important stronghold during troubled times between the Scots and English. There was much activity also during the raids by the Border Revers, the great cattle rustlers that dwelt in the debatable lands between Scotland and England. The Armstrongs, Elliotts, Nobles etc., possies of horsemen armed with sword, pike and gun, protected with helmets and breastplate went through these northern lands burning, butchering men, women and children, stealing cattle and causing mayhem wherever they went for many, many years.

The city centre is particularly attractive with its pedestrianised square surrounded by hanging baskets of the most beautiful and varied blooms. At the north end of this square is the old town hall and clock tower, now the tourist information centre. Very old buildings dating back to the 15th century flanked the town hall and beyond these stands the great cathedral. Five miles to the SE of the city are the prettiest of villages on the banks of the heavily wooded river Eden – Weatheral, Great Corby and Warwick and some six miles further up the river the ancient village of Armathwaite. The whole of the Eden valley is most picturesque, the area is steeped in history and has been the scene of conflict from time immemorial, Hadrian's Wall being proof of that.

Leif Einarsson retrieved his cycle after paying over the odds for its repair and, after we had dined in town, we set off for the Eden valley where I was able to conduct the boys on a guided tour of this lovely part of England. The next morning was again sunny and the two Leifs went with Liz and the children to the meeting, while I lay back as I was still rather tired from our long run on Friday. On their return we were all invited to Liz's mother's home for dinner and tea. What a feed she had prepared! So the Lord's day was pleasantly spent. On Monday morning we said our goodbyes and left the comfort of the caravan for the open road and within six miles we were cladding ourselves in oilskins and doing battle with our old enemy the wind. We arrived at Penrith, a quaint, charming little town on the edge of that delightful area called the English Lake District. This part of Britain must rank as being one of the most beautiful with its majestic, lofty peaks, wooded, holmed lakes, pretty villages and small towns, lovely gardens, attractive homes and grand mansions, these with their own vast acres of tree studded parklands, and streams abounding with trout and wild fowl. In this little town we enjoyed our "twel"(morning cuppa) in a small café, hot sweet coffee and cream cakes; rested and refreshed we set out again. The worst part of our day's journey was going over "Shap". Once again the rain lashed horizontally at us with a force eight gale. At its summit we rested on the lee side of a telephone substation and drank two pints of coffee and ate the sandwiches which Liz had packed for us. Our steep descent into Kendal was dangerous for the wind was such that we were nearly blown off our bikes and blinded by the rain and spray from lorries all hurtling down this steep incline. At Kendal I got a puncture and as the weather was so bad I took it to the small cycle shop where the proprietor soon mended it, but to my surprise he put the tyre back on the rim with tyre levers. I thought to myself, I hope he doesn't nip the inner tube. Two miles outside Kendal my worst fears were realised for my tyre was again flat and from there to Lancaster I was constantly pumping up the rear wheel. The day brightened up as we arrived at Lancaster, the town seemed to be getting a much needed face lift but I cannot say we were much taken with it, and as the day was far spent we decided to look for a bed. Although we had only done a little over seventy miles, as each one of them had been a tough mile and we were very wet and weary, the unanimous decision was to go no further that night.

At the tourist centre we were directed to a cheap hotel and on our way, as we were pushing our bikes up an incline, we met an Irish gentleman who enquired where we were going; on telling him proudly we were heading for the Railway Hotel, his merriment knew no bounds. He laughed most heartily and when able to speak told us that up until the previous week that place was a doss house for down and outs, but its proprietor had suddenly gone up market, put a sign over its shabby door and called it "Railway Hotel" and was hoping to make his fortune. We enjoyed the joke but despite his pleadings to keep clear of the doss house, we parted from our distinguished, jovial, Irish friend.

When at last we arrived at the said dwelling I enquired from the woman that answered the door what price its plutocrat was asking for the esteemed presence of our trio to grace his establishment. On hearing the voice of a prospective lodger, the plutocrat in person came onto the scene, stating the price was £14 each, take it or leave it. So I said I thought £10 was fine, and we would be happy enough at that. He said, "I said £14"; I said, "If you come down two pounds, I'll come up two and we'll call it £11 each". At last we settled for £12 each and everyone was happy. The only other lodgers or guests (I don't like the word guest when one has to pay for the privilege of being called a guest, so I'll stick to lodger) were a honeymoon couple from Canada.

We got on well with the portly old proprietor but his wizened old wife (if she was his wife for I saw no ring), took an instant dislike to the three of us. She was likely expecting gentlemen in top hat and tails, not three scruffy knaves, to their illustrious emporium. The poor soul liked us less when our ever hungry young friend Leif kept asking for more toast, more milk, more bacon, and more marmalade at breakfast the next morning. Once we had acquainted ourselves with the layout of this rather large old building, we set out for the town to dine at the nearest five star chipper. Three fish and chip suppers, three cans of coke, a look around the city and off to bed but not before we had made coffee and I had related the following event.

A little girl had gone to the toilet and had locked the door but, on trying to unlock it she couldn't turn the key and began to cry. Her parents hearing this came to the door, telling her just to take the key out of the lock and push it under the door and they would unlock it for her from the outside of the bathroom; she would then get out. But the little child was so upset she couldn't do it. The father then borrowed a ladder and as the window was slightly open he rescued his little daughter. He put back the ladder and when the girl had stopped crying, they took the child back to the toilet and showed her how to take the key out of the door. Once she had locked it, for it was harder to unlock than to lock, and the girl had mastered the extraction of the key, they told her to push it under the door if she could not get out. This she did and the three of them then found they were locked in. After much shouting a passer by saw something was amiss and phoned the police. They in turn called the fire brigade and all three were rescued. The moral of the story is to make sure you have the key on the right side of the door!

Lo and behold, the next morning at 6am I, being in a single room with a yale lock, came out of my room with the key on the dressing table, pulled to the door and locked myself out and had to wake up the "Lady" of the house. She was not amused and told me that 7am was early enough for any guest and she didn't need me to disturb her sleep. I apologised most humbly and trusted she forgave this foolish old fellow. The reason for my early rise, for the earliest the good lady of the house would condescend to make breakfast for us was 7.30am, was to mend my slow puncture, which I did satisfactorily. After waking the boys, they crowded into my small room, for in it I had the luxury of a shower. While they indulged themselves in their daily ablutions I got the kettle on and we drank tea and had our daily read of the scripture until 7.30am, when we then descended from the lofty heights of the uppermost suites of this very tall gaunt building into the dining room. After breakfast we bade our host goodbye, he wishing us every success on our long journey and a hearty invitation to come again. I fear this feeling of friendly affection towards us may not have been absolutely unanimous, but we left in good humour and we would certainly be inclined to stay there again if ever in Lancaster, for he was an amicable soul and with all her displeasing looks she fed us well, so what more can we say of our short hilarious stay at the Railway Hotel.

On with the oilskins, heading into the southerly wind and away we went; what a climate Britain has, no wonder the invading Roman legions are said to have longed with deep yearning for the warmth and sunshine of Italy as they patrolled Hadrian's Wall, harassed by the Picts, snow, hail, wind and rain; one can sympathise with them. We made good speed that day despite the inclemency of the weather, encountering few hills but plenty of flat uninteresting countryside, most of it thickly populated. By the time we had reached Warrington at 5pm the rush hour was in full swing, but being cyclists we did the obvious thing at every tail back by running down the inside of the lines of cars, or we took to the pavements if these were not too crowded.

On the outskirts of the city, we stopped at a general store which boasted a take-away section. The store was managed by two outstandingly beautiful young girls about seventeen years, plus an old man, the grandfather of one of these delectable creatures. By the time Leif Einarsson and I got out we were beginning to have grave doubts whether young Leif would be accompanying us any further along the road, for both these girls took an uncommon and an amorous liking for this handsome young Faroese man and had not other customers crowded in, there would have been a strong possibility of only two of us finishing the course. Who knows if we had passed by a year later, the store may have carried the name of Leif Av-Reyni above its door. At last young Leif came out, with a grin on his face and a distinct sparkle in his eye, laden with hot pies, pastries, and groceries.

One hundred yards further on we came onto a large school playing field surrounded by a high fence. Once we had scaled this we settled down to a well-earned meal in the early evening sunshine. As we waited for the kettle to boil on the gas stove, the two Leifs pondered the road map, coming to the conclusion that we should have taken the A56 at a roundabout in the city. We now found ourselves on the A49 which meant we would have to cycle an extra four miles into Chester, but this was to be well rewarded, for some miles from this beautiful city and from the summit of a high ridge (and I may say a hard climb), we had one of the most glorious panoramic views we had so far seen. It truly was worth the extra miles cycled, for before us lay the loveliest surreal countryside with its little hamlets, forests, rivers, and far to the NW the waters of the Mersey.

The kettle boiled, the tea was made, we then feasted and drank for a whole hour, having had nothing other than a cup of coffee and a chocolate biscuit since breakfast. At last we stirred ourselves, clambered back over the fence and noticed a large notice stating: "Trespassers on this property will be prosecuted", I thought what a blessing we hadn't noticed it before we clambered in!

We did not stop again until we arrived at the Chester youth hostel, having left the A49 at Cuddington for the A556 which led onto the A54 then onto the A51 into Chester, having covered ninety-two miles for the day. The youth hostel was a magnificent 18th century mansion on the outskirts of the town. No doubt the country-seat of some landed gentry connected with the vast cotton industry of the NW of England. One could only imagine what it must have been like in its heyday, with its vast hall, wide stairway, dining room, sitting rooms, library, its splendid balcony above the hall, the ceilings in each room a work of art in themselves. As one stood there, one was transferred back to an age of wealth and elegance, when the nobility of the area would have rolled up in their gilded carriages drawn by beautiful well-groomed horses. All now overtaken by an age of pollution, speed and noise. In one way I feel that the light pollution is one of this ages worst afflictions; children growing up in Shetland know nothing of the splendour and beauty of the night sky. Today if there are two houses together then there has to be a street light which at once blocks out all the radiant splendour of the vault of heaven, a dimension of vision and wealth of heavenly knowledge unknown to many. Thankfully neither Sullom Voe flare stacks or streetlights affect our view of the heavenly scene above Vatnagerd yet. I thank God for a measure of isolation free from light pollution so far.

I had booked us in at the hostel by phone, as there is no guarantee of a bed if one turns up on spec, as we were to learn the following evening at Ludlow. As Chester is a great tourist attraction most of the young people at the hostel were from the four corners of the globe, with our friends from Down Under being in the majority. Australian and New Zealand young folk all seem to converge on the "old Country", which I think is very fitting, as a lot of their ancestors had their roots here at one time and, as far as the New Zealanders are concerned, a great many have their roots in "Da Auld Rock" (Shetland). The next morning was spent in the town, it is a Roman city planned and built in the first century AD by the Romans as they expanded their empire northward. The river Dee flows through the city and in those days and, of course, much later it was an important port. It is a walled city from which (as in the case of York) one gets a grand view of the city and the countryside beyond it. It is about one and three-quarter miles around the walls. The old centre of the city is most impressive and quite unique with its two levels of shops – one at street level and the next level up is connected by galleries or balconies between the shops. All being built in the black and white half timber style, I would think around the 16th century. The three of us were quite charmed with the beauty and antiquity of the whole place and could have easily spent three or four days exploring in and around this beautiful city. Although we intended only a quick look we did in fact spend the whole morning there, not leaving until after lunch.

Reluctantly we took our departure and headed south through some of the most beautiful rural scenery in England. Its old world beauty and charm was beyond description. The hawthorn hedges were a bridal veil of white, with equally spectacular pink blossom on the wild cherry trees, also the blossom of the horse chestnut and others all along our way. Bird song filled the air, the chaffinch, robin, thrush, yellow hammer, linnet, blackbird, greenfinch and a multitude of others added to this wonderland of exquisite splendour. Many of the little cottages along the way were the half-timber type, so recently admired in Chester. Some also being the thatched variety, having seen many generations come and go, being the abode of family after family with all their joys and sorrows, their births and deaths, their successes and disasters and at last to lay it all down and be carried to their "long home" as Ecclesiastes chapter 12 verse 5 puts it; and their "mourners go about the streets" and they that follow must "number their days and apply their hearts unto wisdom" if they are to find a fairer and eternal country, beyond the beauty of this.

Chapter 8
On to Lands End and Scilly Isles

From when we left Warrington until we arrived back in Shetland we never saw another drop of rain and had sunshine all the way. Added to that blessing we had the wind at our backs right to Land's End in Cornwall. I had said to my companions that once we crossed the Bristol Channel and headed west, this fine northerly breeze would not help us, but I was so very wrong for the morning we altered course to the westward after crossing the River Severn (Bristol Channel) the wind veered round to the east.

After covering fifty miles that afternoon from Chester, we called a halt at a little hamlet called Dorrington and here we rested on a seat set back from the road on the village green, in front of an old memorial to some battle or other. Across the road stands an ivy covered cottage and on seeing this young Leif's desire was to get a few stick insects, slip them in amongst the ivy and start a massive stick colony. Church Lane runs alongside the gable of this ivy cottage and leads to a quaint little country church with a bell tower and striking clock which strikes the quarters and the hours most pleasantly. We had taken the A41 from Chester and then changed onto the A49 at the little town of Whitchurch. All the way down to the River Severn on the English side of the Welsh border one is seeing England at its most beautiful, no wonder the poet has written, "Oh to be in England now that April's there". The prettiest part of our day's run had been around Church Stretton with wooded hills on either side, little hedged fields with every type of tree in all their late spring glory – ash, oak, elm, poplar, copper beech, beech, larch; what a lovely scene it made, the larks in the heavens and thrushes in the high trees.

Onward we sped in high spirits, whizzing along with the northerly breeze behind us until we entered the ancient town of Ludlow, having covered seventy miles since 1pm and having had three breaks along the way. We fancied we had done well, none of us felt in the least bit tired and intended having a look around this town before turning in. We made our way across the River Teme over a very old narrow stone bridge to the youth hostel which overlooks this fast flowing crystal clear river which comes bursting out from the thick cover of a wooded hillside. To our dismay it was full. Back across the bridge we made our way until we found a B & B on the main cobbled stone street. Leif Einarsson spoke to the lady regarding a night's stay. She wanted £16 each but when he told her that young Leif and himself were doing this cycle run for charity she reduced it to £13, asking why I wasn't doing it for charity also. I told her one reason was I did not like asking people for money. She kindly charged me the same as my colleagues. The cottage dated back to the 10ᵗʰ century and was mentioned in the Domesday Book. The Domesday Book was written in 1085 and about that period this cottage was a small inn which was always used by the male relatives of any man or woman brought to Ludlow to be hanged, for there had been a gibbet behind the cottage. In olden days they would lodge in the inn and after the execution, the following morning the relatives would take away the body for burial.

This old town had been very prosperous, being the centre for the wool trade. Its prosperity still showed itself in the grand old houses, many dating back to medieval times; there are also the remains of a red sandstone castle of great bulk which dates back to the very early years of the Domesday Book. After looking around this interesting border town, we smelt out a fish and chip shop and added to the profit of that successful business by purchasing a fish and chip supper each which lasted us to the very door of our historic dwelling. Once in our bedroom, for we all shared the same room, we made much tea and coffee before showering and falling into bed.

I then related the true story (I don't like the word story in relation to truth, especially scriptural truth so I will use "true account" instead), of the origin of the name "Yokie" as in Yokie's burn which flows down the steep face of Sandness hill. This account goes back over 200 years, when the laird of Papa Stour, the small island west of Sandness, was riding home from Lerwick after attending to some business affairs in that town. It was the month of October and the two previous days had seen a great deluge of water from the heavens, so much so that the burns were in full spate. As Mr Henderson, the said laird, rode over the wooden bridge at the Brig-O-Fitch he thought he heard a faint cry. Looking around he could see nothing and was about to ride on when again a feeble cry came to his ear. He dismounted and peered under the bridge at the swirling torrent and there, to his great amazement, he saw the white and terrified face of a young boy about nine years of age, hanging onto the structure of the bridge for all he was worth. Mr Henderson quickly went to the lower side of the bridge knowing he would be unable to pull the boy up against the rushing water on the upper side. Lying on his belly across the bridge he was able with great difficulty to grab the poor child's arm, bidding him to relax his hold on the structure. Once he obeyed, Mr Henderson hauled him clear of the water onto the bridge. Once the frightened boy's distress subsided he was able to relate what had happened, how he had slipped into the burn further up stream and been swept down towards the sea and certain death. As he had passed under the bridge he managed to grab hold of some of its timbers and hang on, and had Mr Henderson not come when he did all would have been lost. The laird saw that speed was essential if the shivering child was to survive his ordeal. On enquiring where he lived and what his name was, he pointed to a poor low thatched house some distance away. To his other question he was able to tell him he was Yacob Nicholson. The laird mounted his horse taking Yacob up in front of him, making all speed for the house. On his arrival and entry he saw a scene of abject poverty. There, gathered around the peat fire in the middle of the earthen floor with their widowed mother, huddled six half-starved little ones younger than Yokie. Their father had been lost at the haaf (fishing in open boats carried on then around Shetland at a distance of forty to fifty miles off shore, Da Far Haaf).

The widow quickly busied herself stripping the child and wrapping him in a blanket before the fire while hearing of his narrow escape. After his clothes were dry and the distressed widow had given the laird and Yokie tea and an oatmeal brönnie, the laird sat and pondered on the situation. At length he said to the woman, "If you are willing, I shall take Yokie with me to Papa Stour and bring him up as my own, he will be loved and well cared for and I shall see to it he gets an education, he will of course be a great loss to you, but had not providence guided my steps this day Yokie would have been dead hours ago. The boy will accompany me on my visits to Lerwick and I shall leave him with you on those occasions. Besides this I shall give you a little assistance on my visits." The weeping mother poured out her sincere thanks and every blessing from God above upon him for she knew, had it not been for this turn of events, they would be in the poorhouse within the next few weeks. Yokie was a sensible boy and having been party to the discussion agreed to go with the laird. After a tearful farewell they left the little home. Henderson, as good as his word, placed a sovereign in the poor mother's hand and made off on their journey. Yokie did well in Papa Stour and by the time he was eighteen was doing all Mr Henderson's business for him at Lerwick, always staying a night in the old home, also bringing along the little relief the laird sent his mother.

On his return to Sandness, prior to crossing the Papa Sound, he would often be compelled to spend a night or two awaiting passage to Papa Stour. On these occasions he would stay at a small house on the Norby links occupied by an old woman and her daughter Barbara, who for a few pence would lodge stranded travellers. On one occasion Yokie found Barbara in the midst of packing her few belongings and on enquiring what was going on, was told that she was leaving Shetland the very next day to seek her fortune in Scotland. "Oh no you're not Barbara, for I deeply love you and will never let you go, for you must marry me". To this impromptu proposal she at length agreed, for she also was very fond of Yokie but, as she was eight years older than him, she feared she had no chance. So glad was Yokie that his proposal was accepted that he ran from the house and leapt over the "doggie hole", a large basin in the Norby burn, where unwanted dogs and cats were put into a weighted bag and drowned. The width across it being 12ft; this is the only time on record that this hole has ever been jumped. Yokie and Barbara settled down at Silerdykes under the shadow of Sandness Hill very happily, working the croft and doing business for Mr Henderson. Yokie is reputed to be the first person in Shetland to try surface reseeding; he threshed out the seed from his hay, carried up tons of shell-sand from the Melby beach, sowing the grass-seed over a hard barren part of the croft then spread byre muck upon this, then spread the shell-sand over the lot with amazing results.

He was also a very fine singer, fiddle player and precentor at the Kirk. Yokie would always go around the place whistling some reel tune or other. Barbara being a very Godly soul and very averse to dancing would scold Yokie, stating he would one day rue his worldly folly by starting the singing in the Kirk to one of his dance tunes. Shortly after Barbara's scolding they were at the Kirk together when her prediction came true, the minister gave out the name of the Psalm to be sung, and to Yokie's lasting disgrace, he started it to the tune of "The cock marched-owre-da midden". He lost his much loved job of precentor and was banned from the Kirk for a month, worse still his beloved was much hurt by his unbecoming blunder. But things mended and they lived happily on for a few years, when suddenly Barbara died, this devastated poor Yokie. All the drive, vigour and panache was gone, and though he married again some years later, to a woman from the Neap at the east end of Sandness, he was never the same buoyant, lively soul he had been with his Barbara.

Shortly after his marriage he was casting his peats in the month of May, when he slipped and ran the feather of his tushkar (tool for cutting peats) into the calf of his leg. This turned to blood poisoning and he died, and was buried beside his beloved Barbara and all that is left to remember him now is a burn named Yokie's burn.

When I awoke the next morning a blackbird was singing so very sweetly outside our window, through which the sunbeams were streaming in from among the ivy leaves growing partly over the upper part of the window, making a moving pattern on my bed. I lay content, just absorbing the beauty of the morn, before the moment that I knew the bed and I must part. How quickly that moment seemed to come, though I must have lain there for twenty minutes or more, I thought so is time in the life of any one of us, so very speedily gone. My sixty-three years had gone, as a tale that is told, a brief moment.

At the breakfast table next to us sat a man of about forty. I think he was a teacher and very interested in what we were doing, he himself had been a keen cyclist in former years, and was able to give us advice with regards to our crossing the river Severn. We thought we would not be able to cross at Chepstow, for it is a motorway crossing there. We were intending to make a forty mile detour via Gloucester, but he assured us that there is a cyclist and pedestrian path alongside the motorway over the river on the same bridge which in time we found was the case.

We followed the A49 through the little hamlets and villages in the sunny morn, the perfume of blossom and flowers being constantly with us. As we sped on through Leominster I thought what strange names and what history must lie behind these English villages that we pass through, such as Hope-under-Dinmore, Moreton-on-Lugg, Pipe and Lyde to mention but a few, as we made our way down to Hereford. Once at Hereford we had a cup of coffee and a look around. Hereford is a very ancient town, being the capital of the Anglo-Saxon Kingdom of Mercia and steeped in history. The 11th century cathedral is well worth a visit, and houses hundreds of chained books including 8th century copies of the Gospels. I suppose the county is best known for its Hereford cattle, a white faced beef breed, and of course for its cider. I expect the town's rise to prominence is due to the agricultural wealth that has ever flowed into it from all around.

From here we set off for Monmouth, again along the A49 but we branched off onto a quiet country road (A466) still being enchanted with the beauty of creation in all its fullness around us. What a magnificent view we were about to enjoy, after a steep climb to a place called Llancloudy. At its summit we gazed back the way we had come, there lay the town of Hereford amidst a patchwork of countryside, dotted with villages, woods and farms. Streams and rivers appeared like ribbons glistening in the sunlight. All around us we glanced over mile after mile of strikingly superb landscape. We sat down on a bank at the side of the road, amidst the hum of bees, busy in their endless search for nectar, the chirping of young grasshoppers, the buzzing of many insects, all at one with us and the rest of nature. We lay propping up our heads drinking coffee from the flask.

Then we mounted our iron steeds and rode quickly down into Monmouth and on through the beautiful Wye valley, passing the spot where fifty-two years previously my father, twin brother and I had camped between the road and the river on a cycling holiday in 1942. Once we had set up our tent and dined, my twin brother John and I tried our skill at fishing and within a few minutes he had caught a 3lb fish, which we ate for our breakfast the following morning.

After passing this spot we were slowly passed by three "Rockers" (bikers) on powerful motorcycles each with a heavy chain across their shoulders. Young Leif was a bit concerned and expected to see them waiting for us around each corner, but of course his fears were groundless and we continued to enjoy our pleasant run as the road wended its way in and out of the country of Wales, following the remains of Offa's dyke, a great earth work built by King Offa of Mercia in the 8th century to keep out the Welsh raiders. It extends from Prestatyn in North Wales to Chepstow in the south. It takes a very winding route and must cover 200 miles in length. One marvels at what has been achieved in ancient times with pick and shovel, hammer and saw, lever and rope, muscle and brain, will and determination. When one thinks King Offa died in 796 at the age of thirty-nine, and was the most powerful King England had known up until then, his claim that he ruled everything south of the Humber excluding Wales, was no vain boast. The very emperor Charlemagne wished his son to marry one of King Offa's daughters, but not before Offa had made sure his son would marry Charlemagne's daughters simultaneously, thereby letting King Offa's power be felt in Europe where he was rightly considered one of the most famous men of his time.

29. Leaving Yate on our way into Somerset.

We said our goodbyes to Offa's dyke at Chepstow and mounting the motorway bridge on the cycle lane, pedalled for three miles across this very busy, noisy thoroughfare. After that we were once again on quiet little country lanes with high hedges all the way to Yate, Europe's largest village. My wife was spending a few days holiday there, at her sister's home, so they made us very welcome. Unfortunately her husband Hans was away on a job in America, as the two Faroese wanted to speak with him, he being a Dane and them being very acquainted with his country. My sister-in-law made us a fabulous meal and after a good night's rest and a hearty breakfast, we set out to the westward with the wind from the east in our backs and the sun strong overhead. We had entered the final phase of our long journey.

Passing through the delightfully named little hamlets and villages of Chipping Sodbury, Pucklechurch, Wick, Abson, Goose Green, Compton-Dando and Temple-Cloud, at length we picked up the A39, leaving our peaceful country lanes behind. We were not long with a following wind in reaching the very beautiful city of Wells, England's smallest city, but not before we had climbed a very high hill. At its crest we rested and drank in the beauty of the panoramic scene before us. To the west the mountains of Wales, also to our right the lovely Mendip hills and the great plain of Somerset spread

119

out like a patchwork quilt, with its hay meadows, fields of corn and beans and hedged pasture land. Wells and Glastonbury lay far below us. The Glastonbury area was once nothing but swamp and water, the town itself being an island. Wells though a city, for it boasts a cathedral, is in fact a small market town with quiet, cobbled streets, all very ancient with lovely old buildings from the 16th century and also a street with 14th century houses near the cathedral. The cathedral is (to use a modern term) "just something other", although I have been to Wells on a few different occasions I am always amazed at this magnificent Gothic architectural wonder, built in the early 12th century. Its west side has around 300 statues, also it has extremely beautiful stained glass windows to say nothing of the interior of the cathedral, which is undoubtedly a wondrous witness to the skill and craftsmanship of workmen that have long gone back to mother earth, for from dust they, as we, were taken and to dust returned, awaiting the rapture or the last summons, 1 Thess. 4 v 16 or Rev. 20 v 12. The two Leifs were enthralled by the medieval clock, this wondrous and unique oddit, had a figure of a man called Jack Blandiver sitting before the clock's bell, at each quarter and hour he strikes, while mounted knights circle Jack and the bell, prepared for battle. Once the bell is silent the knights disappear into the wall of the cathedral, to reappear at the next quarter hour.

While we explored this mighty building we hurried back to the clock each time it neared the quarter hour intervals. There is much to see in and around the city. We visited the Bishop's palace with its moat and saw the wise swans which pull a rope that rings the feeding bell when they are hungry. They were surely not needing a feed while we were there for we neither saw them pull the rope or heard the feeding bell. Being somewhat hungry ourselves we made our way into the town and after a snack and an interesting look around we departed. If we had had more time we should have visited Wookey Hole, another wonder deep in the Mendip Hills. My companions had to make do with a description as I remembered it, as was the same case regarding Cheddar Gorge. I always think of Wells as the gateway of the West Country which we were to enjoy all the way to Land's End. From Wells it is but six miles to Glastonbury, another historical place steeped in myth, legend, new age travellers, and hippies. The Glastonbury Tor rises over 500 feet and is topped with a ruined tower once part of an 11th century church. This town is said to be the place where Joseph of Arimathea (John 19 v 38) built a church in the 1st century. I question the truth of that and more so the tale that the mystical King Arthur was buried in the Tor. There were plenty of odd bods male and female in the town but not so many at the top of the Tor. I concluded it was too much like hard work for many of them, it being a very steep climb but well worth the effort for the view was fantastic.

We left the hippies "hidie hole" and cycled on to the town of Street, the home of "Clarks Shoes". The Clarks were a Quaker family and their business was run on Christian principles, great kindness being shown to their workers; they not only preached Christ but more importantly they lived Christ. As did the Cadbury family (Chocolate Cadbury's). All these Quaker families were the same, they lived meagrely themselves but were very open handed to the poor. Fox being the founder they got the name Quaker from the fact that the people quaked under their judgement preaching. Of course, they have had their day and the ones that are left, that I know of, are of a very mild strain, not likely to cause a ripple on the conscience of any sinner let alone a quake.

At length we arrived at Taunton, the county town of Somerset, but were not impressed and after purchasing a hot pie and making coffee we pressed on as the shades of evening closed in upon us. What a beautiful sky on the horizon it was, the palest of pink turning to an even paler orange higher into the heavens, then a lovely turquoise and finally a dark blue at the very crown of heaven. At last we came on an isolated but pretty white-washed farmhouse just off this now quiet road, with the long-looked for signs "B & B" so in we went, it was a small holding of seven acres. At one time it had been a much larger farm. We knocked, hoping desperately there was room for these weary travellers. A very attractive woman of about thirty-five at length opened the door with a shy little girl and boy hanging onto their mother's dress and peering from either side of her at these "unken folk". Yes she could put us up at £12 each. We were to take our cycles into the back kitchen as there had been a lot of stealing going on.

The house had been built in the 1750s and was typical of that era, with stone flagged floors, low ceilings, wood lined walls and leadlight windows. She led the way up a steep flight of dark stained stairs to our very pretty bedroom with a coomb ceiling which overlooked the front garden and small orchard. We thanked her and she left us stating we were her only guests that night. Her husband worked away all week, so I hope she wasn't taking too big a risk with her B & B business. While the boys got the electric kettle boiled for a cup of tea I opened the casement windows to the exotic fragrance of a bed of night-scented stock directly below the window. What a lovely late evening it was, there was still a little light left in the heavens and two or three tiny pipistrelle bats flitted backwards and forwards between the house and the fruit trees, diving and twisting as they flew in their endless effort to catch the many moths that flew about. I was leaning well out of the little window, blocking out the light from the bedroom, the more able to enjoy the beauty all around. Across the road in a large tree an owl was hooting and another at some distance away was answering its plaintive call. Too soon the tea was ready and I retreated back into the bedroom leaving the windows open to the sweet night air and nature's night sounds.

While we drank our tea and munched our biscuits, I told the boys of the time before the war when the late Captain Andrew Sinclair from Westsandwick, Yell, (at that time his home was in Leith, Scotland) had a visit from his cousin; she had never been away from Shetland before in her life and was, in Andrew's words "very countrified". He arranged to meet her at the Waverley Station in Edinburgh, she having travelled down from Aberdeen after disembarking from the steamer that morning. She duly arrived and Andrew decided to take the tram down Leith Walk to his new home. They boarded the very crowded tram, Capt. Andrew Sinclair at one end of the tram, his country cousin at the other and off they went. Before long he heard his cousin roaring down the tram, "Andreew – Andreew whaa lives awaay up yondrew?" as she pointed to a high tenement block. He pretended not to hear her as he was a very reserved soul but she shouted all the louder and all the folk were greatly amused at this. At length he told her, "he had no idea and she should be quiet", not another word was uttered for a few minutes, until the same booming voice roared down to Andrew, "Andreew – Andreew dus do tink thy twa cousins will be looking after my twa hens, hame, dus du?" When he was relating all this to his two daughters he said, "Oh if only I had the wit of those two hens, I would have hired a cab and saved the embarrassment."

After a sound sleep I awoke at 4.50am, quietly arose, washed, dressed and let myself out of the back door and into the fresh, dew-laden English morn. The sun was just climbing over the leafy tops of the trees in the wood across the empty road, from which a chorus of bird song was filling the air. I wandered along the edge of a hawthorn hedge, still covered with white blossom, thinking now I saw what the lady of the house meant when she had said Spring came late this year. Well, I thought, it's here in all its glory now. From every blade of grass hung a glistening gem as the early sun's rays penetrated the meadow through which I skirted, along the ditch between me and the hedge was festooned with spider's webs all heavy with dew, at present too visible to lure prey into their enmeshment so the spiders would need to forgo their breakfasts. Her few cattle were all lying half-asleep contentedly chewing the cud, as the faint call of an early cuckoo, far across the fields, came pleasantly to ear. In the next field I had hoped to see a fox making for the small copse, after his night's hunting but it was not to be. I felt as I returned back to the house that the early rise had been worth the effort. My two friends were still fast asleep and, as we couldn't get our breakfast until 7am, I didn't disturb them but made myself a cup of coffee, drinking it while leaning out of our window watching the housemartins on their ceaseless task of feeding their hungry families under the eaves of the roof next to the window. Each time the parent bird flew to the outside of their mud home, several small beaks appeared through the hole of the nest. How on earth the parent bird knows which one it fed last is a mystery to me. Another mystery is how that almost spherical mud nest sticks to the side of a house wall, lashed by thunder spates of hard rain, blown by freak summer gales. I suppose it's just another of our wonderful Creator's marvels.

At breakfast our hostess told us that they were hoping to sell the place and move nearer her husband's place of employment. On hearing this my son-in-law thought that we should both sell our homes in Shetland and buy this old homestead, as Leif was as taken with it as I was. He loved England and would ask my wife Jean what on earth made her leave such a beautiful country to come to live in Shetland with all its bad weather, to which she would with a laugh point at me and say, "it's him". When our hostess returned with our bacon and eggs I asked her if she thought it a bit dangerous running a B & B in this isolated spot while her man was away. She said she always took a good look at the person or persons before she let them in, saying "I'm a good judge of character and you all seemed alright to me last night."

After paying the lady and telling her how interested Leif and I were in her smallholding we departed, and were soon passing through the little town of Tiverton heading for Crediton. The beauty of this lovely hilly county of Devon must be experienced either by walking or cycling to appreciate it to its full. One only gets a fleeting glance from car or coach of "Devon, glorious Devon". We stopped briefly as we crossed a small bridge spanning a crystal clear river. Alongside the bank waterhens swam jerkily amongst waterlilies of yellow, pink and white. I didn't think lilies grew in rivers though this one was slow running. Perhaps someone had planted them, for I doubt if the yellow and pink ones are natives of Britain.

We dined at Crediton and again had a quick look around before heading for Okehampton, marvelling that the wind was still pushing us along through supreme scenery while the sun tanned our bare legs, arms and faces. We were very tired when we arrived at Okehampton and lay in the long grass on a nearby bank while the kettle boiled which we poured into our cups of soup powder; refilled the kettle, boiled again and poured its contents into a pan of powdered tattie; this along with a tin of corned beef was our meal. I had spoken to Michael Browne, a friend of mine, on the telephone the night before, stating that we were hoping to pass through Okehampton the next day, and as he and his wife were in the area they thought they would see if they could find us. An hour later while leaving Okehampton we passed the very bonnet of their car, which was backed into a farm gateway, and as we were not expecting to see them, and Michael's wife, Grace, couldn't convince him it was us cycling past, just because we all had crash helmets on, we never met. So near yet so far. We had now joined the A30 and had thought to call a halt at Launceston (pronounced Lanston) but as it lay one mile off the A30 we

30. In Cornwall at last!

pedalled on; Launceston was at one time the ancient capital of Cornwall. The old language of Cornwall died out about 200 years ago, the Cornish people were or are still the only true Britons left in England. We were now entering Bodmin Moor, a wild stretch of beautiful high country, which gave us some lovely views of the surrounding countryside. We stopped for a late tea outside Belventor after a long climb; refreshed and strengthened we moved on and finally came into the town of Bodmin, having cycled just over 90 miles that day. We were not greatly impressed with the town though its history goes back to before the days of William the Conqueror, and it is also mentioned in the Domesday Book. It is likely quite interesting but we were now tired and very hungry. We found a cheap B & B, unloaded our bikes and chaining them together in the back yard we set off in search of our supper, which at length came in the form of king ribs and chips for young Leif, and fish and chips for Leif Einarsson and me. After this we wandered around, being told that if we were to climb Beacon Hill we should see both the coasts of Cornwall, but being weary we declined the offer. Back at the B & B we drank tea and coffee and I told the boys of my trip from Shetland to where we were living in England at that time, just after the war, and called it the account of "An Uncertain Journey".

Towards the end of 1948 I left the employment I had as an apprentice plasterer with Willie Fraser, a man from Scotland who had a big contract to build council houses from Lochside to Gilbertson Park, Lerwick. My main reason for leaving was that I had started work there as a joinery apprentice but as Willie had a surplus of joinery apprentices, and no plaster apprentices, he decided that one of us must be drafted into that loathsome trade and as I was the last young fellow employed in the joinery department, it had to be me. To soften the blow, the dear man bought me a trowel and with many fair words, got me into that branch of work which to this day I hate. I was under a hard man from Wick but we had a fine cheery labourer from Cullivoe, Yell by the name of John Magnus Anderson and he and I got on just fine. If it had not been for him I would not have stuck it a week. He had been in the Airforce during the war and I think he served in India, so between tales and songs from Yell and his exploits in the services, he shortened many a long day for me, neither of us caring much for the man from Wick. John Magnus was hopelessly in love with a girl who worked in Taylor's paper shop, whom he later married. They had, I believe, one daughter, so I only saw John during working hours though he lived in the same hut which housed about twenty of us workers plus a very good cook, for as soon as we had our tea he was gone a courting.

I stuck the job and the Wick man as long as I could, that was as long as John's long list of stories old and new were forthcoming but at last they came to an end and he was scratching his head to remember new ones, many of them having been told around the peat fire from generations of folk long ago now gone off this earth; he had a remarkable memory.

I picked up my wages, such as they were, and considered I had just about enough money to get me down to where my parents were then living in England. I had managed to save a few shillings in the previous two or three weeks, once my mind was made up to quit. At that time the steamer left from Victoria Pier, the custom being that crowds came to see her off, many having no connection with the passengers departing but in those days it was the done thing just to see her off. As I knew many of the boys I had been working with, plus the fact that some of my relations would be there to see me off, I thought it only right and proper to purchase a bottle of rum to pass around and this at 12/6d made an enormous hole in the money I had set aside for my journey. Many of the boys that came down to see me off also had bottles and half bottles so after about an hour, when the dockers were about to remove the gangplank I staggered aboard clutching in one hand the remains of a bottle of rum and in the other my few belongings. I was, to say the least, a little under the weather, having been liberally supplied with the contents of a variety of bottles, with a good lacing of my own. After waving at a blur of familiar and unfamiliar faces I made my way forward along the deck; once clear of the lights of Lerwick and the sooth mooth the old *Magnus* began to roll heavily (no stabilisers in those days). Before long all that had gone down my throat with such bravo and boisterous hilarity returned with all the reverse effects plus a 100 percent deflation and demoralisation. Groggily I lost my grip on the rail and sank down onto the now wet deck not caring whether I lived or died, the latter was now the preferred. I think one of the crew tried to move me at one point but getting no thanks for his effort he left. The next thing I remember was crawling down the deck many hours later, very wet and very cold, and did not warm up any until the ship had docked in Kirkwall and the steward was serving out mugs of steaming hot tea plus a baker's biscuit well klined with butter for 1/- a time. I parted so very gladly with the shilling from my now fast receding funds. Never was a mug of tea more welcome or a baker's biscuit more ravenously devoured. When the few of us in the steerage had had our tea, the steward poured the dregs of the pot into my cup but no second biscuit. He surely saw my need.

I now realised I had not enough money to get home, the little I had I determined to hang onto and buy nothing in the way of food. We at last arrived at Leith and I was desperately hungry when I left the boat and felt I could not walk up Leith Walk to Princes Street, so I boarded a tram and paid two pence and stayed on well beyond my fare. After alighting I walked slowly up to the Caledonian Railway Station and into a warm waiting room with a coal fire burning at one end. I found a seat and within minutes I was fast asleep, only to be rudely awakened at midnight by a policeman who was clearing the likes of us out. There were by then about a dozen of us just taking advantage of free accommodation, none having a railway ticket. I think that the station closed at midnight then anyway. A dejected little group of down and outs, one or two women amongst us, made our way down to the Waverley Station and encamped in the now packed waiting room, passengers and hobo's were sitting and lying everywhere, seats, floor, on top of the large table and under it. At about 2am the police came in again and demanded to see our tickets. As there were so many of us they never got around to me again. Several were unceremoniously turfed out into the cold night. Again they came in at about 4am, looked around, and then grabbed two men and hauled them off. They were surely wanted by the boys in blue. A little later one of the drunks that had been snoring loudly on the table top awoke, got down from the table and still in a stupor proceeded to urinate on the sleepers under the table at which all fury broke out and he was at last grabbed and bundled out of the waiting room amidst cursing and swearing. We happily saw him no more.

At 8am an inspector came in and we hobos went out. I had been told by someone during the night that the cheapest way to travel was by coach and there was a coach that left St Georges Square at 10am for Newcastle. I decided to go and see if this was indeed the case. I arrived at 9.30am only to find a large queue already waiting. To the end of this I tagged on and, sure enough, at 10 o'clock an old rattletrap of a bus arrived with "Hall Brothers Newcastle" painted on its side. When I at last paid my fare and boarded there was only standing room left and I felt very faint with lack of food. After some time some of the passengers left the bus and I was able firstly to sit down in the alleyway of the bus and later I got a seat. At last we arrived at the bus station in Newcastle. I was making for the town of Coventry in the middle of

England but I had now only enough money to get by coach to Preston plus 1/- over. Again I paid my fare and this time got a seat and fell fast asleep through hunger and fatigue, having eaten nothing since my baker's biscuit two and a half days before. At Preston I was awakened by the conductor. It was by then, black dark and a very cold winter's night. At that time I had a dear unmarried aunt who had left Shetland to become a nurse, was interned by the Germans in Belgium where she was nursing, released in 1915 and by then was a health worker. She lived in Blackburn about ten miles from Preston.

On leaving the coach I was directed to the stand for the Blackburn bus which was just ready to leave, I asked how much the fare was to Blackburn. I was told 1/-. I gave a great sigh of relief and passed over my last coin and at 10 o'clock I was ringing my auntie's door bell. I cannot express what a relief it was when she opened the door, or no doubt what a surprise it was to her to see this forlorn figure in person of her nephew standing there. She soon had me hustled into the living room and on hearing all my tale of woe set about getting me a large meal to which I did equal justice, much to her delight. Around midnight she showed me to my bedroom and I knew nothing more until I was awoken with tea and toast and informed that breakfast would be ready at 9am. I was lured out of my bed and into the kitchen by the delicious smell of bacon and eggs, sausage and tomatoes, preceded by a plate of porridge. Looking back at what I consumed that evening and morning, there could not have been any of my Aunt's meagre week's rations left (as Britain was still on strict rationing) but she sipped her tea and admiringly watched her kin make up for meals missed. 1.30pm found the two of us at the bus station where my aunt purchased a ticket for Coventry, saw me onto the ancient coach and pushed half a crown into my hand (12½p). She waited until the bus left and I settled down to enjoy the journey to Crewe where, after an endless wait, broken with a mug of tea and a snowball (cake) for a sixpenny bit in a workman's café, I boarded another old bus for Coventry.

The bus droned on through the darkness, crawling up every little gradient as though it was climbing Everest. On arrival at the bus station I was greatly alarmed to see an enormous queue for the last bus that night which passed through the little village of Mancetter which at that time was my home. I had a sixteen mile journey which I didn't fancy walking on a cold December night at 10pm, burdened down with my bits and pieces. I stood and considered what action I should take for I could plainly see that to join the queue was hopeless, for if the conductor could squeeze three quarters of the people aboard, he would be excelling himself, last buses being notorious for grossly over-crowding during and right after the war; so I hung around at the front of the queue with the air of someone seeing a friend off. At 10pm the Midland Red 765 rolled up and the queue surged forward; I pushed into the torrent of people with my Greenheart fishing rod and thrust it through the crowd and onto the side of the bus thus stemming the flow for a second or two, sufficient for me to get my hand on the rail and my foot on the step. Amidst the volley of swearing and cursing and demands to the conductor to get that beast off the bus, the poor conductor was having his time cut out to keep the rest of the queue in order. I made for the back of the bus and by the time the conductor stopped any more folk boarding, there was no hope of getting the offender out of the bus. It was a long time before the conductor made his way through the bus for the fares. When at length he collected my fare he grinned and said he should by right's have flung me off the bus, you young dog. There was a chorus of "get him off, he's the one that jumped the queue". He winked at me and pushed up to the front of the bus again. Nearly every passenger seated or standing was smoking, the air blue in the faint interior lighting, which of course was normal in those days. When the bus arrived at Nuneaton the most of the passengers got off and a few new arrivals boarded and off we went again. The bus came to my destination a few yards from my house, unannounced I entered the house at 10.45pm, much to the great delight of my parents. A meal was soon on the table as I related all the news from Da Auld Rock and my journey down. This modern age with all it's latest communications, speed of travel and lack of family unity has lost the joy, surprise and relief on receiving a loved one back into its circle.

We at last fell off to sleep in the knowledge we only had another fifty-six miles to our journey's end and did not rise until 8am and even then we spent a lazy hour over our "full English breakfast" and were not on the road until 9.45am. I think it was about the village of Ruthvoes that we first had a glimpse of both the Cornish coasts at the same time, the Atlantic and the English Channel. For some time we had noticed the remains of the old tin mines, mostly they consisted of a tall round chimney and parts of the wheelhouse, from which the cage would lower the workers into the bowels of the earth.

The history of English Tin Mining goes back at least 2000 years and maybe much further, who can tell. It was said in Queen Victoria's reign there were over 600 working mines in Cornwall. A big one I later saw situated at the foot of a cliff, was said to have sixty miles of tunnels beneath the seabed. As in the case of all mining, it was a very dangerous occupation, but with the invention of the Davy lamp a lot of the explosions were averted. A statue of Davy is to be found in the centre of Penzance and upon the plinth of it I climbed while Leif Einarsson took a photo of me. We entitled it "Davy the inventor standing on the head of Davy the ancient cyclist".

At Redruth we stopped to sample a real Cornish pasty, the traditional meal of the tin miner. The pointed ends of the pasty were held by thumb and finger of each hand of the hungry miner as he ate the rest. Once finished he would discard the two ends, as his fingers were contaminated with the poison of his work. Of course, we ate every crumb and enjoyed them immensely along with a mug of hot tea. After our break we sped on over hill and dale until we arrived at St. Ives, a most beautiful colourful holiday town, fine beaches, houses and waterfront. It is the great centre for the painters; a famous artist of the last century, Whistler did much of his work here. They say the light here is ideal for painting. He likely set the trend and since his days artists have flocked to this lovely town.

We raced on towards Penzance for there we had promised ourselves a good feed and the afternoon off. The great island fortress of St Michael's mount loomed up ahead of us like a Fairyland Castle. It is a steep climb up to it but well worth the effort. What a remarkable castle home this is with its great hall and panoramic views from every window, its windy turrets and spectacular flowers and shrubs. At low tide it can be reached by wading the quarter of a mile along a causeway, but most folk prefer the small ferry journey. I was sorry we didn't visit it as intended, for on a later trip to Cornwall, I found it extremely interesting, its history goes back to the 5th century and is very similar to Mont St Michel in Normandy.

We stopped at a large supermarket on the outskirts of the town and after having made our purchases we sat on a bench outside this grand place, boiled up the soup on the gas stove and began our meal, which consisted of soup, tatties, peas, chicken and crisps, ice cream and trifle, topped off with fresh cream cakes and coffee. I had expected one of the supermarket officials to point out that we were at a supermarket not a camping site, but other than smiles and nods no-one troubled us. I reasoned that we had bought all this here, so why not eat it on the premises. We were loath to leave our warm sunny picnic area, being somewhat lazy after our big dinner, but at last we made our way into the town of Penzance and after some difficulty found the

31. Davy the inventor standing on the head of Davy the ancient cyclist.

32. Lands' End. Nearly at the end of the peerie bike ride!

youth hostel. Our way led along a fast flowing clear stream in a lovely part of the town. The houses whose gardens ran down to it, had made a wonderful job of enhancing its beauty with a great variety of blooms, grasses, heathers, and rockeries. It was indeed a credit to the district. We took a few snaps which turned out well.

The hostel was large and very pricey, £12 per night, no breakfast and an hour's work forby so we only booked in for one night knowing we could get B & B for that price nearer the town centre. At 6pm we set off for Land's End ten miles further on and with our faithful friendly wind from the east, we were at our journey's end as far as Mainland Britain was concerned. Land's End has a grandeur of its own, rugged, wild and inhospitable, its granite cliffs will be subject to the same onslaught as are ours at home in Shetland with the Atlantic gales of winter. Here at the signpost with its various arms pointing to this world capital and the next, we were photographed by a friendly soul with each of our cameras. After signing the book in the hotel-cum-gift shop, eating an ice cream and taking a few shots with our cameras, we set off back to the hostel with a strong head wind and a setting sun, a remarkably beautiful sight. After cycling for about five miles I became extremely worn out and if I had stopped I doubt if I could have carried on. On arriving at our destination I could remember nothing of that gruelling last five miles other than the road before me and my exhaustion. I wondered at this for we hadn't had a hard day, if one counts the ten miles return from Land's End we had only done sixty-six miles that day. Before we settled down for the night I related the account of a tragedy on the cliffs of Foula, in Shetland.

In years gone by in the island of Foula, it was the common practice to go fowling in the sheer cliffs around the back of the island. As of course this was the case in many other parts of Shetland to a lesser degree. Foula can boast of having the highest sheer cliffs in Britain with over a 1000 foot drop in one part.

Yearly, men and boys would descend these cliffs on ropes to narrow edges in the sheer face of rock, upon which the sea birds by their multi thousands laid their eggs and brought out their young. These eggs and young were harvested yearly as part of the islanders subsistence with no harm done to the bird population. (This is clearly born out in Faroe, where fowling is done on a large scale in those enchanting isles to this day, and the bird numbers are not diminished in the least. If one species has a poor breeding season the cull is then limited, to allow recovery which is normally achieved in the following year.)

In Foula the account is given of a father and his two sons being engaged in this occupation, and having descended a sheer face somewhere about "Da Kame", busied themselves in their egg gathering along a narrow edge. At length, once sufficient eggs had been collected, the signal was given and their bounty was hauled up to the cliff top by the men above. Those below began their ascent up the cliff face, the oldest son taking the lead, and the father following up behind the younger brother. All appeared to be going well as they climbed hand over hand and ever nearer to the top, until the eldest son saw to his horror the rope above him beginning to give due to the excess weight. Strand after strand of the lay could be plainly seen to be parting and he immediately cried down to his brother, some twenty feet below him, "cut away Daa or I'll cut away the two of you, the rope is giving". Without a seconds hesitation, the youngest brother drew his knife from his belt and cut the rope below his feet. His father, some ten feet below him, looked up in sheer terror and unbelief at the fate his sons were condemning him to, and before he could utter any protest, he had been launched off into space, while wildly flaying the air around him with one hand, still clinging desperately to the loose end of the rope with the other as he hurtled down to his death. The younger brother stated later that he watched as his father fell hundreds of feet to his death on the rocks below. His words were, "I cut away faather and saw him plunge to his death, his "puddens" splattering out upon the klets below like kirnmylk on the but-end floor, but at least Turvald and I were spared."

On awakening the next morning I was feeling fine and once our work duty was by we headed into the town centre, and under the stern, stony, gaze of the statue of Mr Davy high above us we dismounted our faithful steeds, dismantling same by taking out wheels, turning handlebar fore and aft, taking the pedals off and finally packing them in cardboard which we obtained from a motorcycle shop. All this was carried out in the middle of the town opposite the post office at the side of the road. This caused some interest to the many bystanders, who obviously thought we were going to set up a stall and sell cycle parts, as one of their number came over and asked what time the sale would be starting. This was much to our great amusement and had the Post Office refused to take our bulky parcels, we would likely have had to sell them bit by bit or whatever. We at length carried our bundles into the post office for posting up to Shetland. An elderly gracious gentleman weighed and measured them and though he said they were really over the acceptable measurement, he made an exception after he heard how far we had come. We had also packed and forwarded the rest of our proil (gear, booty). We now were free of all encumbrances.

On our way into the centre of town, young Leif had noticed a B & B at £13 per night so had booked us in for that night at least. We explored the town at leisure, enjoying a hearty meal at 1pm. As the day was very hot we found a shady place on the waterfront and watched daring young teenagers (none above fifteen years old) jump off the seawall, which we estimated to be about eighteen feet high, into the sea which at that time was no more than five feet deep. As these boys and girls feet touched the water they jerked themselves backwards and entered the shallow waters like a knife at about a 50° angle. How they didn't do themselves harm I don't know but as the tide further ebbed they at last gave it up. On my last visit to Penzance some years later there was a notice forbidding jumping or diving from the seawall. I trust none of these brave amazonian maidens or lionhearted swains had come to grief. Just before 5pm we bought tickets for our trip to the Scilly Isles which lay about twenty-five miles west of Land's End. The following morning found us enjoying the two and a half hour trip to St Marys, our final destination.

I noted we had had nothing but sunshine since leaving Chester and again that day that great orb was out in all its splendour. As we proceeded along the coast a commentary from the bridge informed us of the places of interest, such as the skerry of Mousehole (what a quaint name for a fishing village) where a hermit lived for many, many years; also along the coast is the place where all the transatlantic telephone cables come ashore.

The Isles of Scilly was a wonderful place for our journey's end and once ashore at Hughtown, Leif Einarsson hired a tandem but young Leif preferred to lie on the hot sand surrounded by pretty girls. We found the island very attractive and coming to an old cottage festooned with flowers of every kind, Leif wanted to stop to get a photo. As this was being done a very old woman came out and invited us to see her back garden, which could only be described as a miniature "Kew". Leif was enthralled with all this for he loved flowers. On hearing that we had cycled down from Shetland she told us she thought her great grandfather came from there. He had been caught by the press gang and put upon a man-o-war as a young boy but when they had anchored off Hughtown he had managed to swim ashore under the cover of darkness and hide until the ship had gone. He then settled and lived the rest of his life in St Mary. As I said afterwards to Leif "she certainly looked like an old Shetland body". Before we left she dug up and cut off a variety of plants for Leif which at length found their home in his garden at Waas. What a culture shock they must have had! It was only about six or seven miles of road that St Mary could boast of but how pleasant that run was. A tandem we found was far easier to propel along and would be the ideal machine for a long trip.

When we returned and told young Leif of all we had seen, he hired a cycle and sped around the isle not wanting to be outdone. After this we dined and explored until we had to return to the ship.

The next morning, our cycling trip finished, we headed for the bus depot and boarded the National Express coach for Aberdeen. A daily run of twenty-two hours. Once settled in young Leif promptly went to sleep. Leif Einarsson rushed from one side of the coach to the other photographing the lovely scenery. I bade my two dear companions farewell when we arrived at a town outside Plymouth called Saltash, there I had arranged to meet my friends Michael and Grace Browne for I was to holiday with them at their home in Bath.

The night after our arrival home in early July I climbed to the top of the Hoddans, quarter of a mile NE of Vatnagert, our house. The late hour and steep climb were richly rewarded as I gazed over the idyllic scene before me. The great St Magnus Bay, some twelve miles across at its widest, lay like a millpond. The flash of Eshaness lighthouse flashing every thirteen seconds, the dark outline of the northland dominated by the broad sweep of Ronas hill some 1400 feet high. The sky above this scene being the palest pink backed by a clear sky of purple backed again and blended into a dark blue. The occasional bird flying off to a belated roosting place, the stillness only being broken by the cry of the shalder (oyster catcher) which strangely seems to be in keeping with da hömin (twilight). The silhouette of the ewes lying on the tops of knowes between Veltigert and the Ness loch. A lamb standing on the very back of its dam, stood out clearly even from this distance. In the nearby lochs an odd trout böls. So still are the waters that the little ripple from the trout can be seen widening to the very extent of the loch. A white mist clings to the surface of the Colaster loch and to the SSW the waves of cottonwool-like mist roll down the steep face of Sandness Hill. I see an odd light shining from the window of this house and that, still being light enough to distinguish the colour of the homes except our own house which is black and has now blended in with its dark surroundings. To the east, Snarraness and West Burrafirth voes appear as long luminous figures separating the dark cliffs on either side stretching far inland, like mini fjords in Norway. Mist tumbling down the face of the sheer cliffs of the Neon. A rabbit hops through the damp grass, its little white tail now being the only thing visible as it bobs up and down getting further from my vision and fainter until it has gone. It is coming on to 1am and within an hour a new day will dawn, the hömin will once again be swallowed up by the increasing light, so I turn for home, thankful to a gracious God for His preserving care over His wayward child and those that have ventured with him on our spin through Britain.

My companions and I planned to cycle from Moscow to the Siberian side of the Ural mountains the following year but as crime in Russia was becoming so great we were advised not to go. If at a later date things settle down in Russia I'll maybe try it, but for the meantime we had better sign off.